MORE PRAISE FOR QUIETING THE MONKEY MIND

CW00428855

"Having herself benefitted from their beautiful music, my friend Naomi Judd told me about the husband and wife team of renowned musicians and purveyors of peace, Dudley and Dean Evenson, and shared, 'you need to know these two and their music.' So I did just that. I invited Dudley and Dean to perform live for some of my guided group meditations. As I discovered for myself, along with my workshop attendees, their musical gifts are immeasurable. The collaboration was beautiful and raised the experience to a higher level. Meditation with music can truly be transcendent. With their book, *Quieting the Monkey Mind*, Dudley and Dean transcend traditional teachings and skillfully guide us to disconnect from the noise of life while helping us make a deeper and more peaceful connection with ourselves. Their profound collective wisdom shared within these pages is what we can all benefit from to better understand the benefits of meditation, music, and for achieving the harmony we all seek."

—JOAN BORYSENKO, *New York Times* bestselling author of *Minding the Body, Mending the Mind*

"Music has been at the core of my being all my life. Amidst my personal and professional busyness of family and career, meditation is a practice that I need and can never have too much of. But, making the time, and getting to that 'quiet place' is sometimes a challenge. Well, help has arrived! My longtime friends Dudley and Dean Evenson, renowned musicians and creators of tranquil and peaceful music, have written a beautiful book that teaches meditation and the value of incorporating music into your practice. Deep, thoughtful, and overflowing with the wisdom and loving spirit of these two amazing souls, *Quieting the Monkey Mind* is the required bridge to travel in helping you achieve a deeper state of quietude and personal transformation."

—NAOMI JUDD, Grammy Award-winner and bestselling author

"Music pioneers Dudley and Dean Evenson's beautiful and beneficial book, *Quieting the Monkey Mind*, carries an important message that is timely, refreshing, and indispensable for readers and meditation practitioners of all ages. Welcoming music and sound to the silence is a profoundly helpful approach to deepening the practice and sacred art of meditation. This book will help you embrace peace within the stillness."

—LARRY DOSSEY, MD, author of *One Mind*
— BARBARA DOSSEY, PHD, RN, author of *Holistic Nursing*

"A beautiful book! Filled with information, exercises, illustrations, and photographs that bring illumination to the reader on the subject of meditation and music. Dudley and Dean Evenson have written a wonderful how-to guidebook that explores the world of yoga and sound in a way that is both user-friendly and impactful. With practical tips and techniques to enhance your energetic essence and well-being, *Quieting the Monkey Mind* is truly a blessing."

—JONATHAN GOLDMAN and ANDI GOLDMAN,
authors of *Chakra Frequencies* and *The Humming Effect*

"Inner peace, compassion, connection, and selfhood...meditation is paramount to achieving these qualities. How can we bridge our modern life, based on pace, not peace, to the meditative state? The answer lies in this wonderful book, written by musical and mindfulness geniuses Dudley and Dean Evenson. Let them accompany you on the journey through *Quieting the Monkey Mind*, as you learn how to use tools including breathing, postures, mantras, affirmations, toning, trance rituals, instrumentation, and more to unveil your 'clear light mind,' your essential self, through the musicality of meditation."

—CYNDI DALE, author of bestselling books
The Subtle Body and *The Complete Book of Chakras*

"This is the book I needed many years ago when I first began meditation. I was not one that could just sit and be. It was through music and sound that I strengthened my practice, and now I enjoy all of the different types of meditation that Dudley and Dean present in their beautiful book *Quieting the Monkey Mind*. I couldn't think of better teachers to guide you on your journey through meditation."

—MADISYN TAYLOR, co-founder of *DailyOM*, and
bestselling author of *Daily OM: Learning to Live*

"Pioneering musicians Dudley and Dean Evenson, have gifted us with *Quieting the Monkey Mind*, a valuable tool that teaches us how to unburden our minds, relax and re-center ourselves with meditation and music. This extraordinary book offers timely lessons on how to be quiet, providing the perfect antidote to the often chaotic and noisy world in which we live."

—JACK CANFIELD, bestselling author of *The Success Principles*™ and co-author of bestselling *Chicken Soup for the Soul*® series

"The spirited, dynamic duo of Dudley and Dean Evenson have spent their lifetimes exploring the arts, creating music, spreading peace, expanding consciousness, and healing the spirit. Now, with their ever-timely book, *Quieting the Monkey Mind*, you can learn the valuable and life-enriching music-infused tools needed to calm the mind and rejuvenate the body through meditation. The ancients knew the benefits of this sacred process, as do Dudley and Dean. Well-honed wisdom shines through these pages, and the helpful guidance to a more peaceful and blissful state is manna for the soul."

—ANTHONY J.W. BENSON, creative business strategist and consultant, injoi Creative

"As we know from ancient healing traditions, there is nothing more sacred than word put to sound. And there are few in the world as qualified and inspirational to bring this work forward like Dudley and Dean Evenson! I've been a longtime fan of these two music pioneers for years and have used their beautiful songs for healing and in workshops. This easy-to-follow book will delight, soothe, and regenerate the soul in a gentle, yet impactful, way."

—DEANNA MINICH, PHD, health and wellness advocate, author, and nutritionist

"*Quieting the Monkey Mind* is a compact instruction manual for beginners. It is filled with precise and practical guidance on how to integrate toning, mantra, affirmation and breath work into your daily practice. It is authentic and lucid because the authors are themselves advanced practitioners and have a lifetime of sustained practice and rich experience to share with those starting out on the journey."

—JAMES O'DEA, author of *Soul Awakening Practice* and other works

"What mastery put together by Dudley and Dean Evenson in their book *Quieting the Monkey Mind*. The sacred practicing of sound and meditation, as shared by two lifetimes of knowledge and a world of sacred traditions. I love this book!"

—CHRISTINE STEVENS, MSW, MT-BC,
author of *Music Medicine* and *The Healing Drum Kit*

"*Quieting the Monkey Mind* is a helpful guide to many methods of meditation to enhance one's life. From mantras to mindfulness, affirmation, breath, sound, and creating sacred space, this beautifully photographed book is inspirational and reveals how meditation is accessible and so worthwhile for raising one's frequency to deep inner peace."

—BRIGITTE MARS, author of
The Country Almanac of Home Remedies

"As a certified spiritual mentor and teacher of meditation, I highly recommend Dean and Dudley Evenson's *Quieting the Monkey Mind* for those interested in meditation, especially utilizing sound and music in their practice. With a market overwhelmed with meditation books, this unique guide is fresh with new information to enhance one's meditation technique. From explaining the importance of breath and mindfulness, toning to activate the chakras, using bija Mantras, affirmative singing, trance meditation, and healing with drums, to their production of music and sounds that facilitate deeper meditative understanding, *Quieting the Monkey Mind*, offers keen insight into the importance of sound in the process."

—REV. Z. MELINDA WITTER, spiritual mentor
and meditation teacher, Witter Consulting

"Dean and Dudley Evenson have created in *Quieting the Monkey Mind*, a beautiful and accessible guide to rediscover our diamond-self through music and contemplation. As a practitioner of sacred sound, I know how powerful the combination of music and meditation is in reaching our authentic self. Bravo!"

—DIÁNE MANDLE, author of *Ancient Sounds for a New Age*,
Tibetan bowl recording artist, and educator

"Sound meditation is profound, as it conveys the depth of the heart. With the excellent book *Quieting the Monkey Mind*, Dudley and Dean awaken us all to the peaceful beauty within."

—ED AND DEB SHAPIRO, authors of
The Unexpected Power of Mindfulness & Meditation

"*Quieting the Monkey Mind* freely gives over 40 years experience and hands-on knowledge of meditation, music, toning, chanting, mantras, bowls, bells, and other sound tools. Dean and Dudley Evenson are pioneers in the alternative spiritual movement that began in the '60s and continues to this day. Not only will you learn a lot about meditation and music, you will have a peek inside the lives of these talented souls as they traveled the country in their bus in the 1970s. This grounded handbook is born from well-lived lives and anyone interested in meditation would be wise to acquire and use a copy. You'll share in their wisdom as well as in their heartfelt commitment to bringing more joy, peace, and love to our planet."

—KRYSTA GIBSON, publisher *New Spirit Journal*

"*Quieting the Monkey Mind* is a perfect guidebook for the modern age. Music and the meditation go hand in hand, and music completes meditation with its divine beauty and allows you to recognize your essence. This exciting book will assist you to know your inner self and to realize the outside world much better."

—SERGE KOZLOVSKY, author of *Nourishment of Soul:*
Mantras and Meditations for the Contemporary Woman

"I have been teaching meditation for 44 years and practicing since the age of 12. Some days I get caught up in my monkey mind. I find some of the exercises given in this excellent book to be extremely useful to bring me into space, into the void. As I practice the teachings shared by Dudley and Dean Evenson, I can awaken to the deepest place within myself. I recommend *Quieting the Monkey Mind* to everyone, including beginners and long-time meditators."

—LIGHT MILLER, Ayurvedic doctor,
author of *The Divinity Within*

"Having survived a challenging and tough early life, I now approach my life with drive, faith, gratitude, and a passionate sense of purpose. With writing books, hosting a television show, speaking, teaching, and more, I am often a woman in perpetual motion. I also understand the value of bringing peace and harmony to the whirl of my busy world and meditation and music help me achieve just that. Having, over the years, had the pleasure of experiencing the musical talents of Dudley and Dean Evenson from their amazing albums, and even more so when they provided beautiful music at my events during my guided meditations, I am excited by the release of their book *Quieting the Monkey Mind*. Dudley and Dean share their collective knowledge and teach us how to better achieve calm amidst the storm, quiet our minds, and find the inner peace we all need and deserve. I hold these two amazing people in high regard, honor their many gifts, and am incredibly grateful that not only myself, but many more individuals will experience their wisdom, benefiting all those who seek quietude, and read this fantastic book."

—IYANLA VANZANT, bestselling author of *Trust*
and host of *Iyanla: Fix My Life*

"As a musician and meditator who has used sound and music to go deeper into both worlds for over 50 years, I applaud the release of this highly accessible and much-needed how-to guide. *Quieting the Monkey Mind* offers a broad spectrum of concepts and techniques that can be of benefit to experienced or beginning meditator, musician, and non-musician alike. I encourage you to buy this insightful and helpful book and give it to your friends, library, and schools."

—STEVEN HALPERN, Grammy-nominated
recording artist and author of *Sound Health*

"*Quieting the Monkey Mind* by Dudley and Dean Evenson has a beautiful grace and flow. It is at once intelligent, visual, historical, poetic, and informative. Anyone wishing to establish a meditative practice will have a wealth of information and suggestions from which to draw. Truly a lovely book."

—AMARI MAGDALENA, wisdom keeper and author

"I have just finished reading Dudley and Dean Evenson's delightful book *Quieting the Monkey Mind*. I have meditated for years practicing qi gong and other forms of meditation, and I have to say I learned a lot from this guidebook. I greatly appreciate the way they weave history, faith, and science into this important work."

—HILDA BOOTH, psychotherapist and qi gong teacher

"*Quieting the Monkey Mind* is a beautiful and empowering offering to any of us searching for a more centered, peaceful, and expansive life. Dudley and Dean Evenson have gifted us with an easy-to-read guide filled with exercises and information, supported by inspiring stories and photographs that engage the reader. The self-healing power of the human voice through speaking, chanting, toning, and singing is revealed in ways that one can benefit from immediately. With great compassion, Dudley and Dean expand the traditional notion of meditation so that one may effectively personalize their spiritual practice. I love their ongoing mission of spreading 'Peace Through Music.' I highly recommend this guidebook!"

—JAMES K. PAPP, author of
Inquire Within: A Guide to Living in Spirit

"Dean and Dudley Evenson are seasoned meditators and take anybody from the beginner's mind to a seasoned meditator through the various modalities and levels of mindfulness into a deeper understanding. Their leadership and work at Soundings of the Planet, the people they have encountered in their lives, and the inner and outer journeys they have been on have been phenomenal. Highly trustworthy!"

—ILONA SELKE, creator of the Dream Big Summit
and author of *Dream Big: The Universe Is Listening*

"Dudley and Dean Evenson have done it again with *Quieting the Monkey Mind*! Everyone needs tools to harness the untamed part that lives inside our mind, the part that won't let go of the chatter and come to a place of peace. This book, along with the countless selections of soothing music that this creative duo have produced, will do just that!"

—CAROLINE SUTHERLAND, Hay House
author of *The Body Knows* series

QUIETING THE MONKEY MIND

HOW TO MEDITATE WITH MUSIC

DUDLEY EVENSON & DEAN EVENSON M.S.

QUIETING THE MONKEY MIND:
HOW TO MEDITATE WITH MUSIC
Copyright © 2018 by Dudley Evenson and Dean Evenson

Creative Director: Anthony J.W. Benson, injoiCreative.com
Cover Design by Bob Paltrow Design
Meditation Figure Art by Elijah Evenson
Original Soundings Mandala by Dean Evenson
Book Design by Bob Paltrow, Anthony J.W. Benson, Dudley Evenson
Photos by Dudley Evenson unless otherwise noted
Photos of Dudley by Dean Evenson & Brett Steelhammer
Photos of Dudley and Dean Evenson on pages 23, 150 and
back cover by Tad Beavers, Peter James Studios
Art/Illustrations on pages 21, 28, 47, 57 and 103 by Bob Paltrow
Editors: Paul Russell, Cami Ostman, Jane Harris, Sarah Guitart, Brett Steelhammer

Printed in the UNITED STATES OF AMERICA
ISBN-10: 0-9991379-0-5
ISBN-13: 978-0-9991379-0-1

Library of Congress Control Number: 2017918324

Published by:
Soundings of the Planet
PO Box 4472, Bellingham, WA 98227
www.soundings.com

For press inquiries, email:
music@soundings.com

NOTE TO READER: This book is intended as an informational guide. The approaches,
tools, and techniques described here are meant to supplement, and not to be a substitute for,
professional medical care or treatment. They should not be used to treat a serious ailment
without prior consultation with a qualified health care professional.

"*Music is the harmonious voice of creation;*
an echo of the invisible world."
~ Giuseppe Mazzini

CONTENTS

*"The more you listen, the more you will hear.
The more you hear, the more and
more deeply you will understand."*
—Dilgo Khyentse Rinpoche

FOREWORD

Deep listening and creative modulation of rhythms, tunes, and songs have been employed by humans since the beginning of time as a source of delight, synchronization, recalibration, and refinement of consciousness. This gentle hacking of our brains has also been brought about by lullaby-singing mamas, inspired musicians, ancient shamans, and modern DJs. While such experiences can occur spontaneously, they can also be intentionally cultivated through the practices of meditation introduced in this valuable guidebook.

This precious treasure that you hold in your hands is the distillation of years of deep listening, study, practice, meditation, creative experimentation, and research by two of the world's leading experts. They share the many ways that music can inspire meditation to refine, harmonize, and expand human consciousness. Drawing insight from over 100 combined years of research and exploration with some of the world's wisest and inspired musicians, mystics, contemplatives, and techno-savvy souls, Dudley and Dean Evenson have skillfully composed this creative guide for using music as a tool for enhancing meditation. They offer sage advice for integrating meditative practices of sounding, chanting, mantra, affirmations, kirtan, working with singing bowls, and many other creative methods to expand the self-tuning options you can bring to life.

For half a million years, humans have been singing and creating musical sounds to elevate their consciousness and convey the depths of their feelings, complex visions, and experience beyond words. For tens of millions of years, whales have been singing their songs across the oceans of the world.

While studying the Neolithic cave paintings in the Arcy-sur-Cure caves of France, University of Paris ethnomusicologist, Legor Reznikoff, discovered that the areas of the cave with the highest concentrations of paintings were those in the most acoustically resonant chambers of the cave, located more than a kilometer below the surface. He theorized that the Neanderthal communities sought out these power spots deep in the earth and gathered there to sing and chant in these dark, resonant chambers that served to magically expand the resonance of their voices, imbuing the images they painted with greater meaning and potency.

As our instruments, technology, methods, brains, and communities continue to evolve, humans are becoming ever more creative and adept at using music and sound to alter our moods and to shift our states of personal and collective consciousness. *Quieting the Monkey Mind* offers its readers a brilliant medicine bundle of inspirations for how to participate in this age-old search for deep, meaningful, sonic resonance in our lives, relationships, and world.

While this book will certainly inspire you to learn how to quiet the rambunctiousness of your distractible wild monkey mind and calm your distress, it will also introduce you to a variety of powerful ways to open your heart and mind. It will aid you in discovering and awakening more deeply to the rare and precious human resources of inner peace, clarity, mindfulness, loving kindness, and compassion. You'll learn time-tested methods that have been cherished and passed down for generations from teachers to students across millennia that will now help you to open and expand your awareness to discover extraordinary harmonics of serenity, harmony, unity, connectedness, and beauty that are ever present and available within and around you.

As the great Indian mystic and musician, Hazrat Inayat Khan, wrote in his classic work, *The Mysticism of Sound and Music,* "The true use of music is to become musical in one's thoughts, words, and actions. One should be able to give the harmony for which the soul yearns and longs for every moment. All the tragedy in the world, in the individual and the multitude, comes from a lack of harmony, and harmony is best given by producing it in one's own life."

Quieting the Monkey Mind offers a wealth of practical guidance for developing and sustaining a personal meditation practice with music. For those more experienced in contemplative practice or modern psychonauts who are seeking new ways to refine, deepen, and expand their consciousness, musical practices are offered to help one listen more deeply to the subtle interweaving harmonies of complex waveforms of the music of life. For beginners or for experienced meditators, this book is a jewel with the power and potential to heal the world.

Intentional listening is the key to meditation, music, and mystical wisdom. Some of the Indian musical gurus that we have studied with offer the classical instruction for serious students of music to devote the first year of their studies simply singing the sound 'Sa' (which in Indian music is like the 'Do' or 'middle C' of the Western musical scale). As one goes deeper and deeper into this practice and refines and deepens one's inner listening over time, one comes to realize that all the myriad notes in the musical scale, and all the octaves in an infinite extension, are harmonics of this single note. And as you travel further into the seemingly 'simple' yet profound practices offered in this guidebook, we encourage you to bring a sense of curiosity, open mindedness, and reverence for the wonders that they may reveal to you. As Brother David Steindl-Rast has reminded us, "Another name for God is surprise" – and this book is sure to evoke many resonant surprises for you!

In a recent study from Apple and Sonos, researchers explored the power of listening to music to help people make meaningful connections. The study revealed that on average, people listen to 4.5 hours of music a day at home. And when listening to music the distance between housemates decreased by 12%, and they are 15% more likely to laugh together, 33% more likely to cook together, 18% more likely to say "I love you," and 37% more likely to have sex! These statistics support the belief that we can use the power of music to help us to connect more deeply with ourselves, each other, and the world around us. This connection can happen whether in the intimacy of our own home, with thousands of fellow dancers at a festival with multiple stages, or in work settings where people are grooving to the same tunes while working together. The profound power of music to help us connect more deeply with ourselves and others is amplified through exercises like those introduced in this book, when we learn to listen to music in a mindful, curious, and deliberate manner.

Dudley and Dean Evenson, wise elders in contemplative acoustic science, have done their homework and research, honed their skills, and refined their creative spirits as composers, musicians, performers, videographers, and recording artists. They have generated a vast archive of profoundly potent and moving musical medicine that they have offered to ease the stress, open the hearts, and expand the minds of countless people around the world. As you experience this book, and as you learn to listen ever more deeply, you can rejoice in knowing that you're in resonance with an ever-expanding field of vibrant hearts and minds attuned to the powerful harmonies of inner peace, wholeness, and higher awareness!

Joel & Michelle Levey
Founders, Wisdom at Work • WisdomAtWork.com
Authors of *Living in Balance* and *Mindfulness, Meditation, and MindFitness*
Faculty, University of Minnesota Medical School

Dean Evenson and I are excited to share with you what we have been learning about meditation, its interaction with music, and how it can help improve our lives.

When we first became exposed to meditation many decades ago, we found that it made a powerful impact on our quality of life. Since then, we have continued to practice and learn as much as we could about meditation and its benefits in order to help bring peace into our often less-than-peaceful world. In a way, our story is the story of a generation, the one that came of age in the turbulent '60s, a powerful time of awakening to something that had been hidden deep within us. After a decade of civil rights protests and anti-war demonstrations, our generation knew what we were against, but it took us many years of intense personal seeking to discover what it was that we were actually for.

On a basic level, we were searching for meaning and for understanding, trying to make sense of this crazy world we were born into. We didn't accept the status quo and we yearned for a living truth. We asked a lot of questions, and we are still asking questions: What kind of life do we want to live? How can we make the world a better place? How can we help? How can we heal? I am guessing that if you are reading this book, then you are also asking some of these questions.

Facing page (clockwise from top left): Dean before college band performance; Dean with daughters Sarah and Cristen; Dudley and Dean with daughter Cristen (Eva Rainbow) in front of Woodstock tipi; Dudley Dickinson living in Japan; Soundings of the Planet first five cassettes display 1979; Thomas Banyacya, Hopi Prophecy keeper, Tibetan monk, Dean with video camera; Santa Cruz musicians and kids Dean, Dudley, Khabira, Aziz, Sarah, Cristen, Kahlila; Dudley posing for cover of Desert Dawn Song; John Denver and Dean playing at Chief Fool's Crow's 88th Birthday Pow Wow Pine Ridge, SD; Dudley and Dean in Moscow's Red Square on Citizen Diplomacy Artist Ambassador tour; Dudley, Dean and son Elijah in front of Afghan yurt.

In 1968, Dean Evenson had completed his Master of Science degree in Molecular Biology and moved to New York City to find his true path. He had been playing flute since he was 10 years old and although he had studied science, his passion still lay in music. Apparently, his direction wasn't going to involve science at all and judging from his interests, it was more likely going to have something to do with music and filmmaking. Auspiciously, Dean's apartment in Manhattan's East Village happened to be right across the hall from Dudley Dickinson. That's me! We found we were well matched and shared similar creative visions for our lives. It didn't take us long to realize we were going to be together for a very long time.

Early on, our journey encompassed the newly emerging portable video movement. We pointed our video camera where we wanted to learn, and interviewed wisdom keepers who offered ideas that might contribute to a more conscious world. Later, our journey involved the founding and running of our music label, Soundings of the Planet. Life was full and very busy with raising our three children, running a business, and building community around us all the while. For years, we lived and traveled in a half-sized school bus and even gave birth to one of our children in the bus. Our lives together have been quite an adventure to say the least. We share some of these stories elsewhere, but here, in these pages, we want to illuminate the parts of the story that involve the interwoven paths of meditation, music, and spirituality.

When Dean and I met, I had recently returned from traveling in Asia and living in Japan. It was almost by accident that I came upon meditation. My sister, Sarah, was my traveling companion and we had booked a room in a Zen monastery in Kyoto, Japan. As was the custom there, the monks rose at dawn to sit for an hour in silent meditation. They told us we were welcome to join them, so we decided to give it a try. Boy, an hour can really be a long time when you are first trying to sit on the floor with your legs crossed. Getting the body to remain comfortably still was enough of a challenge, but we hadn't even gotten to the hard part: the part about turning off your mind and quieting down the mental chatter. In retrospect, sitting in that temple was a sacred initiation into my path of meditation.

Later, while visiting a small village near Kathmandu, Nepal, my sister and I were exposed to a mantra for the first time. Our self-appointed tour guide was an eight-year-old boy who spoke just enough English to show us around. After pointing out some ancient stone statues and wooden carvings, he demonstrated for us the turning of a Tibetan prayer wheel. As he turned the wheel, he taught us to chant the six-syllable Sanskrit mantra engraved thereupon, OM MANI PADME HUM. We had no idea what a mantra was and also no idea of its significance. We wouldn't learn its true spiritual meaning and purpose for many years.

Soon after we met, Dean became a recording engineer and I worked as a photographer. In 1970, we ended up purchasing a Sony Portapack (portable video camera) and it was a move that literally changed our lives. On the day we bought the camera, Dean lost his job in the recording studio. He also stopped shaving and he never looked back. You'll believe it when you see the length of his beard today! That night, we videotaped The Jefferson Airplane at the Fillmore East, and soon afterwards we began to travel the country with our camera, documenting everyday people as well as the new teachers and gurus who were showing up around us. We naturally became involved in the emerging culture that was appearing in the wake of the protest movements of the '60s.

Along the way, we discovered *Autobiography of a Yogi* by Paramahansa Yogananda, *Integral Yoga Hatha* by Swami Satchidananda, and other spiritual books. We started doing yoga, became interested in a healthy diet, and learned the fundamentals of meditation. We came to realize that there was a whole other world out there quite different from what we had grown up with and that our mainstream culture had gotten a lot of things wrong regarding how we eat, think, and live on the planet. We knew we had much to learn.

Living and traveling in the bus during the 1970s was an adventure in exploring consciousness and we captured a lot of what we were learning on our new video camera. We videotaped gurus and yogis, Native American elders, healers, environmentalists, and many others involved in creating a new paradigm. When yoga and meditation first started coming into public awareness, we began exploring them with great enthusiasm. The ideas and philosophies from the East that we were exposed to resonated with our souls and influenced our music as well. Dean began to play more long, slow tones on his flute, while I discovered special harp tunings that lent themselves to making open, spacious music.

After a decade of traveling in the bus, we eventually landed in Tucson, Arizona and in 1979 we attended a Ram Dass lecture where we had permission to record his talk and sell the tapes. Baba Ram Dass (aka Richard Alpert) had become well known in spiritual circles for studying meditation with his guru in India, and he had written a popular book called *Be Here Now* which caught the attention of many young seekers. After the lecture, we were surprised when we got 50 orders for this *Evening with Ram Dass* tape. We suddenly realized people had tape players at home and were interested in this format. The half-inch, black and white video format we were working with had very few distribution outlets since there were hardly any playback decks in the whole country. Thus, it occurred to us that we might want to put our video aside for a while and focus on making audiocassette tapes of our music that people could actually take home and play.

So that's exactly what we did. In addition to the Ram Dass lecture, we decided to make a recording of the music that was coming through us at the time. One night, Dean went out to sleep in the desert, and the next morning, he set up a pair of stereo microphones and recorded the birds at dawn. He brought the field recordings back to our makeshift studio and we played our flute and harp while listening to the recording of morning birdsong. Our friend, Jonathan Kramer, came in and added his sonorous cello tones and we created our first album called *Desert Dawn Song*. We soon added three more recordings and with those first five albums which included the Ram Dass tape, we started our record label, Soundings of the Planet. We wanted it to be a voice of the planet. By recording the sounds of nature for people in cities to listen to, we hoped to encourage them to be better caretakers of the Earth. We sold our early tapes at swap meets and discovered that people were very attracted to this new form of relaxing music, and our Peace Through Music mission took off.

As we had been studying yoga and meditation, it was a natural fit that we tended toward music which encouraged relaxation and stillness. Initially, we were simply making meditative music from the heart that reflected the peacefulness of the natural world. In the process of our travels, we had been inspired by our contact with Native American wisdom keepers so our music with natural sounds was in support of their compelling message about respecting Mother Earth.

As practitioners of yoga and meditation, we have benefited greatly from the blessings these activities have brought to our lives. As musicians, we see how intertwined the sacred and musical can be. We have been fortunate to study with Indian yogis, Tibetan lamas, Zen monks, rabbis, ministers, and Native American medicine people. With those masters to guide us and using our personal intuitive compass, we delved deeply into this very important field of self-discovery and found that the use of sound, music, and chant can greatly enhance the meditation process.

Now, in *Quieting the Monkey Mind: How to Meditate with Music*, we are honored to share some of the experiences and insights we have had on our path of life, and impart a few of the gems that we have picked up along the way. In this book, we share some basic principles of meditation along with a wide array of sound tools and practices that can be used to take one into deeper states of inner peace and meditative bliss. Find what works for you. The ideas and practices shared here can be of benefit to experienced meditators as well as to those who are just beginning the process of meditation. No matter where you are in your meditation practice, we trust that you will find useful tools and techniques that will allow you to access deeper levels of inner stillness leading to a richer sense of self and personal empowerment.

NOTE TO READER: While most of the music we have produced together through our record label, Soundings of the Planet, carries Dean Evenson's name, Dudley Evenson also performs on the recordings. Although this writing is mostly composed by Dudley Evenson, it is based on content that both of us have discovered, researched, and developed over the years. Sometimes it's hard to differentiate between our voices, but no matter who wrote what, we hope that the material we are sharing here will benefit your meditation practice, your peace of mind, and your inner state of being.

We Wish to Provide Some Useful Answers to These Questions:

What is meditation and why practice it?

What is the difference between prayer and meditation?

Why meditate? What is our goal in inner contemplation?

How do we choose music that enhances meditation?

How do we create a personal sanctuary for our practice?

How should we sit and position our hands?

How do we use breath to focus the mind?

How can we let go of our thoughts?

How do we use breath and toning together?

Why does mantra mean 'mind protection'?

What are affirmations and how can we use them?

How do we create a personal affirmation or mantra?

How does one use a mala, a rosary, or prayer beads?

How can one use Tibetan bowls and bells?

How are kirtan, chanting, prayer, and mantra different?

How is a walking meditation different from a sitting meditation?

What is the benefit of a regular meditation practice?

The word Dhyana in Sanskrit means 'contemplation, reflection' and 'profound, abstract meditation.'

CHAPTER 1
WHAT IS MEDITATION AND WHY PRACTICE IT?

Meditation is an inner training of our mental processes in order to attain a calm state of centered balance, awareness, and spiritual expansiveness.

We can't always control what goes on around us, but we can learn to control how we react to and internalize what happens in our outer world. Meditation can have immense benefits for our spiritual and physical well-being. There are many forms and techniques that have been developed by multiple cultures over the ages to help advance the meditative process, and we will be sharing some of them. Meditation is much more than a relaxation technique, although it does contribute considerably to relaxation and stress reduction.

Through a process of focused concentration, we can attain a quality of mindfulness and compassion that enhances every aspect of our lives. Relaxation and concentration are the first steps, and once we have mastered them, we can go beyond them and open ourselves to the elevation of our consciousness towards an experience of universal oneness. In this guidebook, we will share our understanding of some of the basics of meditation and give you tools that will hopefully help improve your own experience. Specifically, we will be addressing how the use of conscious breathing, music, toning, chanting, mantra, affirmations, and listening to certain recorded music can offer a richer and deeper meditation session.

Why Meditate?
What Is Your Goal in Sitting
Quietly for Minutes or Hours on End
Contemplating Your Inner Universe?

For as many people as there are in the world, there are probably as many different motivations for pursuing a meditation practice. In spite of the subtleties of apparent contradictions, there are several intentions and qualities that people who practice meditation have in common. Here are some that we have identified:

- Meditators want to find more inner peace in their lives.

- Meditators are striving to continually become better people and are seeking answers for how to accomplish that.

- Meditators have an innate sense of compassion for the world that resonates within their soul.

- Meditators are striving to have a connection with something greater than themselves, a higher spiritual power.

These may seem like farfetched motivations to some, but in our travels throughout the spiritual and meditative communities we have visited over the past four decades, we have continually found people who have a great love for humanity and the planet and want to find ways to make the world a better place.

For us personally, meditation has provided a training ground for mental discipline that allows us to keep worry and negativity at bay when we are searching for ways to reach our goals of creating a more peaceful planet. Together we guard against losing our positive sense of being when we confront the challenges of today's world.

As we develop a meditation practice, we find that things which may have bothered us in the past no longer hold sway over our emotions. We feel lighter and happier, and we are better able to cope with stressful situations in our lives. Thus, the effect of the meditation experience extends far beyond the short time we may spend sitting quietly and can help us to live a more complete and fulfilled life.

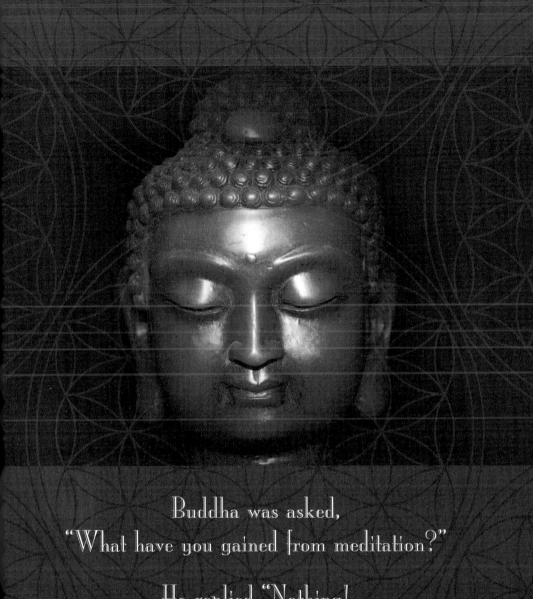

Buddha was asked,
"What have you gained from meditation?"

He replied "Nothing!
However, let me tell you what I have lost:
anger, anxiety, depression, insecurity,
fear of old age and death."

3 Simple Stress-Busting Steps

Even though meditation isn't just about relaxation, it can still be one of the most effective tools we have to help us deal with life's challenges. Modern lifestyles have caused a new kind of stress that our forebears didn't know because of the busy, stress-filled lives most of us live. While our ancestors may have gotten an adrenaline rush from being chased by a wild animal, our demons are often the ones we are chasing in our own minds.

Stress comes in many forms. It could be a relationship conflict in the family or at work, worry about paying the bills, or other things. In any case, how we deal with it is up to us. There are many ways to help a person relax including learning how to breathe, to move our bodies, and to take time to rest in stillness. Music can also be an excellent tool to aid in the process of relaxation and meditation.

We all need to learn to relax. We should know by now that stress or, more specifically, our reactions to stress, can cause detrimental effects in our bodily systems. The resulting tensions may contribute to heart disease, cancer, neurodegenerative diseases, or mental lapses. With that in mind, we would do well to develop some simple stress busting habits.

Here are three simple steps to consider as we start our exploration:

Step 1: Learn to Breathe

Breathe in this day for
it is given to be lived

Breathe in the morning
when the sun rises

And in the evening
when it sets

Always breathe deeply and fully

And exhale completely

Step 2: Move It!

Getting the energy moving through your physical body will help to release endorphins that enliven your mind and lift your spirit. Joyful, free-flowing movement can be a wonderful release to help let go of unnecessary thoughts or concerns. Finding the exercise or movement system that suits you will keep you coming back for more. It is a joy when you love to move your body and have the discipline of regularly doing your yoga, running, stretching, dancing, or whatever your preferred mode of movement is. Go ahead and sign up for that tai chi or yoga class, do your daily run, or get that massage you have been needing. All these activities are good in themselves, and music can enhance their benefits in many ways. We'll go into the different types of music later on.

Step 3: Rest in the Stillness

Know that a prelude of yoga or movement prepares the way for accessing the quiet space within. By way of breathing and moving, your body settles down and the mind is able to calm itself and be ready for the visualizations and peace that can arise when the mind is empty and clear. Music can be a focus to help you center on your own inner sanctum, the innermost place of your being. Just BE. When we are relaxed, calm and peaceful within ourselves, we enhance our health and well-being.

Dean Evenson on Meditation

Meditation is the pathway to the nectar of the soul,
the activator of essence, the process of peace and the place where
God speaks to us in a still, small voice. It is a practice of patiently
letting go of the Me to become one with the Magnificent.

Breathing with awareness allows the mind to be connected to a peace that
fills the body with comfort and well-being. Hope springs from knowing
that all is perfect and we all have our part in this mandala of creation.

Just watch the breath and listen to the rhythm of the quiet heart.
A multitude of thoughts will fly on by while the source of all being swells up
to clear out the cobwebs and gift us with a tingling flurry of free form energy.

What path is there that leads to such ecstasy?
It is right inside and knows no boundaries of blessings.
It is the unfolding essence leading us on through the soft summer night
into the sweet morning light. We give thanks for knowing this.

What Is the Difference Between Prayer and Meditation?

Some say the difference between prayer and meditation is that in prayer we are asking God for what we want, but in meditation, we are listening to what God wants of us. Both prayer and meditation can play an important role in our spiritual practice. One basic prayer that is always helpful is simply asking for guidance. We all want to know the best choices to take so that we may have a productive and fulfilling life, but sometimes we have a hard time figuring out exactly what we should be doing, what specific path we should be following, what job we should take, etc. When we can learn how to quiet our busy minds and listen to our inner guidance, we are more likely to receive inspiration about which steps to take so that we can achieve our goals.

Guidance Meditation

Repeat to yourself either silently or out loud:

I am open to receiving guidance in whatever form it comes.

I am especially open to my higher self or angelic self
so that I may receive divine guidance for the
many decisions I make along the path of my life.

By adhering to my highest principles,
I find that I am in a position to be divinely directed
to make the perfect choices that achieve
the highest benefit for all.

I ask for guidance that will benefit others as well as myself.

When I clear and quiet my mind, I find I am best able
to receive the ideal direction for my life.

Primordial Clear Light Mind

*A more esoteric perspective about
our 'Light Mind' from Ancient Tibet:*

A primordial clear light mind
is something that we all have within us.

It is not something external to us.

It is on this basis that we
can attain enlightenment.

When we can see, straightforwardly
and non-conceptually,
the nature of our clear light mind,
and remain totally
absorbed on this nature
without ever regressing from it,
we have become a Buddha.

—Gelug/Kagyu Tradition
of Mahamudra
(H.H. 14th Dalai Lama)

What Is the Clear Light Mind that the Ancient Scripture Speaks of?

Is it something attainable by us mortals or only available to the likes of the Buddha and the Christ? The truth is that this light exists in all of us, but instead of recognizing it, we allow the veils of the material world to cover the light with a shroud of darkness in the form of busy thinking, worry, and constant mental chatter. Dean loves to point out that modern scientists recognize that our DNA emits light in the form of photons and even on the physical level there is evidence that we are made up of light. So, in essence, the goal of meditation can be to move us closer to seeing clearly the nature of our mind, which is ultimately pure light.

Many people across the ages have been able to access their divine mind through a steadfast practice of meditation. Through meditation, we too can hope to remove the impediments to this light by letting go of that which causes our suffering: clouds of fear, anger, hatred, envy, craving, and self-doubt. As we let go of these negative emotions, we make way for a more compassionate, joyful, and expansive state of being. Through a regular meditation practice, we can expect to reach a state of inner peace and move ourselves much closer to the realization of our divine nature.

As musicians, we have been especially interested in exploring how music and sound can help the meditation process, so in this book you will find many techniques and systems that use sonic tools to enhance the meditation process. Although it may take some time, and of course personal discipline, we hope that the tools offered here can help you in your own life quest.

CHAPTER 2
MEDITATION AND HEALING MUSIC

Overview

Since stress is a constant factor in our lives at just about every level, no one is immune. How we deal with stress determines how happy and healthy we are. Fortunately, there are ways to mitigate the stresses in our lives. Some fun and useful ones involve meditation, music, and sound.

All cultures on every part of the planet, from ancient times to this day, have used music in some way to lift the spirit and to enhance the meditation and healing process. Because of its nature, music can serve as a doorway to the spirit, a bridge between material and transcendent worlds. It also turns out that sound affects us on all levels from the emotional to the mental to the physical. It reaches into our very depths, resonating through every cell and molecule of our being. Therefore, combining musical practices with our meditation practice can be highly effective. Both recorded music and self-generated music and sounds can enhance the journey of going within.

It is interesting to note that healing music became popular around the same time as meditation, massage, and yoga were coming into mainstream awareness. The '70s were a time of new innovations and explorations into healing and consciousness so when a few pioneering musicians began to create a more spiritual and meditative form of music, it was natural that the newly blooming fields of massage therapy and yoga would discover and apply its benefits. The relaxing, soothing music most often used by therapists and yoga practitioners creates a peaceful ambiance for one's process. On a physical level, the slow pace of the music actually helps entrain the breathing and bodily systems to a calmer and more balanced state. Entrainment simply means 'synchronize.'

Much of this book is focused on music and sounds that can be made by the human voice and simple instruments, but first we want to consider recorded music since that is how most people in our modern era listen to music. Today there are many ways to access recorded music including CDs, DVDs, tapes, records, downloads, computers, smart phones, iPods, iPads, tablets, radio, television, cable, and the many internet streaming services available. It wasn't always that way though, and we can remember simpler times when radio was special, television was rare, and a record came in three sizes 78, 45 and 33 & 1/3. Maybe you remember those days too.

Today, however, we have levels of stimulus and input from more directions than people ever had in the past. We can know instantly what is going on anywhere in the world. With social networking sites, we even know vivid details of our friends' lives and their friends' lives. Through the internet, we can read just about anything that is happening locally, nationally, and globally, much of which is 'bad' news. Research and learning are good. We can 'Google' any question we have and receive a multitude of answers immediately. Yet, what are we supposed to do with all this information? We have access to more news and sound bites than we have need of so it is paramount that we learn how to filter it so we are getting authentic information we actually can use and which benefits us. There is nothing wrong with having access to knowledge of many things, but how it overloads our minds and causes stress is something we do need to learn to deal with.

In the '70s when Dean and I were first getting into yoga and meditation, we had a visit from some roving Jehovah's Witnesses who were passing out their literature. The topic of meditation came up, and we expressed our enthusiasm about its possibilities. We mentioned how great it was to learn how to clear our mind and let go of our negative thoughts. They, on the other hand, were horrified and said that an 'empty mind' would allow the devil to come in. That idea surprised us as we felt we already had the 'devil' in our minds and we wanted to get it out! Our experience had been that through the yoga postures, mindful breathing, and meditation, for the first time, we felt like we were actually putting our whole body/being into a state of prayer. We had a sense that through quieting our minds we were attaining a much deeper and more direct spiritual experience. That visit from the 'Witnesses' did confirm for us that people had different perceptions of meditation from ours at that time. Fortunately, things have changed a lot in the 40 years since then, and now many more people across the globe are opening up to the health and spiritual benefits of yoga and meditation.

How Do We Choose Music to Enhance Meditation?

To help clear your mind and enhance your meditative focus, there are many sound tools available. In this study, we will share with you a number of them including toning, humming, mantra, chant, affirmations, and song. Listening to recorded music is also a way to slow down the busy mind and settle into a meditative state. For instance, when you play peaceful music in the background, you can use the slow pace of the music to regulate your breathing, being sure to breathe in and out deeply and fully. As you try to calm and quiet yourself,

most likely you will notice a vast array of thoughts proceeding across the wide inner screen of your mind. What do you do with these thoughts? You can let their random interplay be a disturbing undercurrent of your life, or you can decide to clear them out by focusing on your breath and the music in order to give your busy mind a break from so much thinking. Through meditation, your goal is to slow down and gradually minimize this parade of thoughts.

Soon after beginning our record label, Soundings of the Planet, we began to receive considerable feedback from listeners about how the music had helped them in dealing with chronic pain or illness and even mental issues. We then became curious to understand exactly how the music was working to support the healing that people were reporting. In our research over the years, one of the things that has become clear is that instrumental music without repeated refrains or familiar melodies is the most effective in helping a person let go of their thought processes. Our goal in meditation, or in any healing modality, is to release the constraints of mental tape loops and repeated thought patterns. The music we were creating flowed more like nature and it seemed to be just what people were wanting to help deal with the stresses in their lives. We also discovered that because sound is a carrier wave of consciousness, the intention of the musician who created the music is very important. At the same time, the intention of the person listening to the music also influences the effectiveness of the music.

For entertainment, we may choose music that is familiar, enjoyable, or that gets us up and moving, but when we want to select music to help deepen our meditative or healing experience, we are going to be looking for something different. Thus, we choose peaceful, ambient kinds of instrumental music that will be more supportive of healing and meditation. Music of flute and harp can be especially meditative and the addition of high quality recorded sounds of nature can also create a sense of peace.

One thing to be aware of is the quality of the music itself. Since music is an art form, the innate beauty of the piece is significant and how it resonates with you. We want to steer clear of 'formulaic' music as in the concept that 'Slow Music + Nature Sounds = Healing Music.' Very often this generic type of music can be irritating and boring. In our meditation and healing process, we are aiming to uplift our spirit, so music with a real sense of peace and joy is beneficial.

We find that as much as we enjoy listening to classical music, it is not ideal background for meditation because of the often intense musical expressions that show up in the middle of a symphony. Such sounds can be very shocking when one is trying to quiet down and go deeply within.

Often the slower andante and largo sections of classical music are sad or moody which also may not be supportive. Classical music is known for its repeated themes which are designed to engage the mind, and so it isn't helpful in letting go of thoughts.

Through our research and the feedback we received over the years about our music, we came up with these simple principles that apply to music that supports both healing and meditation:

- Slow rhythms entrain bodily systems
  (heartbeat, pulse, digestive system, respiratory, muscles)
  to a more natural rhythm.

- Natural sounds (if present) give a sense of peace.

- Tones are nurturing, clear, warm, and gentle.

- Pace is slow but with a sense of joy and beauty.

- Music doesn't have hooks and
  repeated refrains that engage the mind.

- Feeling is more like nature, flowing.

- Sub-audio frequencies (if present) entrain brainwaves
  to Alpha or Theta state.

- Intention of both the musician and listener is important.

Other kinds of music do use repetition and that can be an aid to meditation. Devotional chanting, sacred music, or trance music are designed specifically to take one to a deeper place spiritually so there is a benefit to the repetition. Tuning into a mantra or the resonance of a chant can be helpful to relax the mind's attachment to mental tape loops and incessant thinking. Whether one chooses relaxing ambient music or more engaging vocal, chant, or rhythmic music, any can support the goal of clearing the mind and letting go of internal dialog and other mental chatter. With all that being said, everyone will have their own preferences of music that helps them center and clear out thoughts that impede contemplation.

Listening Suggestions for Meditating with Recorded Music

- Find a quiet place where you will not be disturbed.

- Make yourself as comfortable as possible.

- If you can, dim the lights in your area.

- Use headphones if available for a deeper experience.

- Close your eyes and imagine you are in a peaceful place in nature.

- Take a deep breath followed by a long exhalation.

- Continue the slow breathing while listening to the natural sounds (if present).

- Follow each musical line separately identifying the instruments.

- Let the music and the natural sounds merge.

- If you are distracted by runaway thoughts, bring your attention back to your breath and the music.

- Remember, meditation takes practice and even though the mind may wander at first, eventually it will become easier to focus.

- Return to this state of peacefulness often.

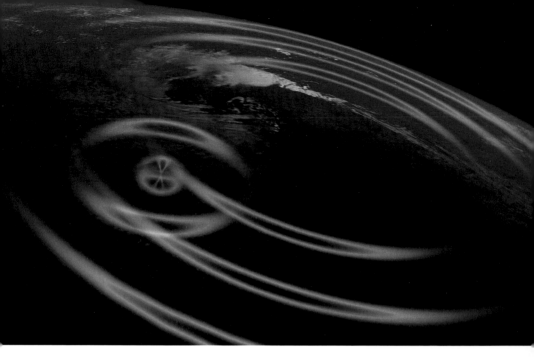

Earth Resonance Frequency, Entrainment, and Brainwave States

Ever since he first learned about the Earth Resonance Frequency (ERF), Dean has included its subliminal vibrations in his recordings. His interest in science and how things work led him to appreciate the benefit of mixing this natural frequency under the music as a carrier wave of nature itself. The ERF also happens to coincide with the frequencies our brains emit when we are in the peaceful Alpha or Theta brainwave states. Here's a somewhat technical overview of ERF and how sound in its many forms can influence our inner state of being.

In this section, we're going to talk about frequencies in a very subtle sense. Sound is the vibrational environment that affects our auditory system. The apparent range of audible sound is described as the frequencies of vibration that occur between 20-20000 cycles per second or Hertz (Hz). This extends from very low sounds such as the deep pitched growl of an avalanche, to the very high-pitched whispers of foam on the ocean. One end elicits a sense of power, the other lifts us to the heavens. The spread is incredible to feel and behold. Music exists in this vast range of audible sound and, along with numerous factors, affects us in diverse ways.

Our physical body is affected by vibrations even when they are below the range of hearing. One such ultra-low frequency (ULF) is called the Earth Resonance Frequency (ERF). This frequency of our beautiful planet is located fundamentally at 7.83 Hz. There are several factors at play here, and we will share our understanding of the scientific basis of resonant frequency and then explain how that ties in with our states of consciousness. We will also describe how the ERF or other ultra-low frequencies can be used in music to support reaching a meditative zone more easily.

First of all, any space, whether it is a room, a bottle, or a cathedral, has an inherent resonant frequency. If you sing a variety of tones into a room, there will be one primary tone that will sound louder in that specific room. If you blow across the top of a bottle, there will be a tone created that depends on the size and shape of the space inside the bottle. These are the resonant tones or frequencies inherent to the room or the bottle, the resonant frequency of the space or cavity. A flute is a perfect example of this principle since by pressing a key and changing the size of the chamber that the air is blown across, the pitch or frequency of the note is changed.

Now let's look at a much larger space – the atmospheric cavity that surrounds the Earth, that spherical donut of air that is between the Earth itself and the ionosphere. This vast space also has its own resonant tone or frequency which happens to be 7.83 Hz. This exact frequency was predicted mathematically by a German physicist and professor named Winfried O. Schumann in the 1950s. What he calculated by using the size of the Earth, the atmosphere, and other factors has since been corroborated via modern instruments.

The Schumann Resonances (SR) are a set of spectrum peaks in the extremely low frequency portion of the Earth's electromagnetic field spectrum and are global electromagnetic resonances generated and excited by lightning discharges in the cavity formed by the Earth's surface and the ionosphere. The primary of these frequencies is always around 7.83 Hz. This frequency also happens to be the wavelength that dolphins, whales, and crickets communicate on. Also, our nerve cells fire at close to that frequency. From time immemorial, all life systems on this planet have been bathed in this drone of nature's own frequency.

Now let's look at how the ERF relates to us and our meditation practice. As you may know, our brains emit ultra-low frequency sound waves that vary depending on the state of our consciousness. When we are in our busy, rational frame of mind, our brains emit Beta frequencies in the range of 14-30 Hz. This is called our Beta brainwave state, and occurs when we are active and thinking, doing computer work, driving a car, or something that requires left brain or rational thinking. We need to access this state to function in the world on a daily basis.

When we are seeking a space to meditate or heal, we want to drop down into the next state which is deeper and more relaxed, so we enter the Alpha state. This is when we are awake and alert, but also peaceful, calm, and centered. The Alpha range is around 7-14 Hz and is a very safe state to be in because one is still aware and alert to the surroundings but also open and receptive to being at peace and accessing our more intuitive faculties.

When we want to go even deeper, we drop down into the next state which is called Theta and the frequencies our brains emit at this level are around 4-7 Hz. Theta is the state of deep meditation, inner quiet, and various trance states. Deeper still is Delta at about .5-4 Hz and occurs when we are in deep sleep, or in a coma. REM sleep can sometimes be in Beta because even in dreamtime, the mind is active and possibly having a nightmare eliciting Fight or Flight mode.

BRAINWAVES

BETA   (14-30 Hz)
Rational, Left Brain Thinking, Concentration, Busy, Active, Awake, Engaged

ALPHA   (7-14 Hz)
Peaceful, Calm, Centered, Relaxed, Healing Receptivity, Dreamy, Light Meditation

THETA   (4-7 Hz)
Deep Meditation, Inner Quiet, Trance or Altered States, Bridge to Subconscious

DELTA   (.5-4 Hz)
Deep Dreamless Sleep, Unconscious, Coma

So how can tuning into the Earth Resonance Frequency help us reach a deeper state of meditation? The easiest way to access the ERF is to spend time in nature away from man-made frequencies such as the 60-cycle hum of electronic devices and other frequencies that are found in cell phones, computers, traffic, and the many transmitters that surround us in our modern lives. It is difficult to experience the ERF in cities with all the modern sounds and noises, so we sometimes add this frequency to recorded music. The way this works in the recordings is through a process called 'entrainment.'

Entrainment is simply the synchronization of an organism with an external rhythm, essentially two bodies vibrating together. Fast music will entrain us to its rhythms so that we want to dance or move. Music with slower rhythms or no apparent beat can entrain our body to relax, and even positively affect our heart rate, digestive system, and nervous system. That is entrainment on a larger, more physical level. The ERF and other ultra-low frequencies entrain at the more delicate level of our brainwaves, our state of our mind, our consciousness. We don't take this subject lightly because it is about reaching into our inner depths.

Adding the Earth's own natural frequency to our aural ecosystem can be one more pillar of support on our meditation path. While nothing can surpass the peace that comes from simply being in nature, at least having the ERF available can help mitigate the intensity of modernity. Dean explains that in our Soundings of the Planet studio, they place the ultra-low frequencies subliminally under recorded music or sounds of nature. This is done through a process called amplitude variation, and is not heard with the ears but rather felt or sensed by the brain itself. Other companies use a system called Binaural Beats which transmits separate frequencies on different speakers. If the two frequencies are 7 Hz apart, the brain then hears the difference of 7 Hz. Of course, this only works if you have two speaker sources. Both systems have been shown to be helpful in moving to a deeper, more relaxed state in preparation for, or as part of, one's meditation practice.

CHAPTER 3

HOW DO WE CREATE PERSONAL SANCTUARY?

My Sacred Laundry Room

Ultimately, the personal sanctuary we have the most intimate access to is within the confines of our own inner awareness, but because we live in a physical world, we can benefit by finding or creating an environment that will best support our meditation experience. When possible, select a quiet place where you will be undisturbed for a little while. If this is not available, any place will do. Experiment with what works for you. People have been known to have meditative experiences in bathrooms, parks, subways, and just about anywhere.

The picture at left shows our laundry room that we converted into a meditation and yoga room. I call this 'My Sacred Laundry Room.' I also record a lot of my videos here for our Soundings of the Planet blog and You Tube channel. We want you to know that you can make any place into a holy sanctuary for your meditation. It could even be in a closet, in a corner of a room, or somewhere outside.

Initially, it is ideal to set aside a specific place to meditate where you can put together a small altar, light a candle, and maybe burn some incense if it agrees with you. If you don't have space to dedicate a whole room for your meditation practice (and most people don't), then designate a corner of your bedroom, another room, or even a closet where you can create a sacred sanctuary for your practice. By adding a few meaningful pictures, books, crystals or other elements, you help designate this as your special place for quiet contemplation. These visual images and special objects can also serve as a focus to gather your wandering mind and draw you back towards your spiritual center.

If you have a Tibetan singing bowl, a crystal bowl, or even a small bell, they can be used to set the tone for your process and their resonance can be a simple way to introduce music and sound into your practice. You can also play peaceful, recorded music during your meditation.

For meditation, you can either sit on a pillow on the floor or in a chair or stool, depending on your flexibility and comfort. It is preferable to sit upright, but lying down is okay if a physical condition requires it. Otherwise, sitting up will yield better results and keep you from the tendency to fall asleep. Meditation involves relaxation of the body, but that is not its only goal. Through the meditation process, one is aiming to attain an acute clarity of mind. Obviously, falling asleep doesn't support this aim. A man at a recent workshop complained that he was continually falling asleep during his meditation. It turned out that he was meditating while lying down, and he became so relaxed that he would naturally fall asleep. We gave him some helpful and wakeful tools to use involving breath awareness, mantra, toning, and using a mala or prayer beads. We'll speak about these tools later in our discussion.

"As the moments of bliss increase in direct relationship to the amount of time I set aside for relaxation and meditation, a formula is developing in my life to allow, indeed to encourage, more time to seek the infinite source of creation within myself. As I open up to creation's miracle of life, the time set aside for the restoration of my personal energy becomes the cathedral of keeping my connection with the infinite open, vibrant and joyful, coming from the place of stillness deep inside. Find the time to relax and love this life we have been given and you will find your true self." —Dean Evenson

Meditating in Nature

Meditating in nature is also a good idea. Creating a small shrine in your yard, or sitting in a quiet area like a public park can support your practice. If you can't find any particular place to meditate, you can do a 'walking meditation,' which we'll explain in another section. We don't, however, recommend meditating in the car if you are driving! But if your car is parked, then meditating in the car can give you some quiet privacy. Dean and I often sit in our car for a few minutes when we come home from a busy trip to town and there we enjoy a quiet moment before having to get out, unload the groceries, and go into the house where all sorts of things are waiting to be done!

Posture, Posture, Posture!

How Should We Sit and Position Our Hands?

People in the western world often have pretty bad posture, partly from leaning back in chairs and couches, or slouching over their computer terminals. Therefore, Westerners rarely straighten and strengthen their spines. Are we becoming a spineless nation? In the East, people are used to sitting on the floor, and so they develop a stronger spinal column. In any event, if you want to enhance your meditation experience, we recommend you sit on a cushion on the floor, cross-legged, and with your spine erect.

The half-lotus position with the legs folded with one ankle on top of the other thigh, is good and not too difficult. The full lotus position with both ankles on top of opposite thigh takes more practice and is difficult for most people. If you use a chair, try not to lean on the back but rather hold yourself upright through the strength of your spine. Imagine that each vertebra is stacked nicely, one on top of the other, and visualize that there is a string of light pulling you up through the top of your head. You do not want to be stiff or rigid, but stay flexible and fluid, even in this stable and upright posture. In this position, your head is held high, your shoulders are relaxed, and your lungs are expanded.

There are several ways to hold your hands. One way is to place your hands in your lap, palms up with one hand resting gently in the other. It is best not to grasp or interlock your fingers because that tends to create unnecessary tension in your hands and arms. Another way is to hold your hands close together with the fingers pointing downward toward the floor, palms facing toward your body. Your hands can also be in a prayer position, although holding this position for a long time may be difficult. Your hands could also simply rest, palms down, on the tops of your legs.

A common way is to let the hands rest on the legs, palms facing upward, with fingers open toward the knees. If you want to increase the connectivity, let your thumb and first finger touch. This position creates a complete circuit within your body. There is a whole system of hand positions called 'mudras' that can direct mental focus towards various virtues that one wants to enhance. But for now, simple is better, so sit with your hands in whatever position is comfortable for you.

Setting an Altar of Intention

The picture above shows the windowsill by our kitchen sink. It provides a nice focal point to elevate the energy of our daily chores.

We like to create altars in many places, especially so that we can use our daily tasks, like washing the dishes or doing the laundry, as opportunities to be mindful and focus on our spiritual essence. Setting an intention for your meditation practice or for your upcoming day can also be a beneficial habit to get into. This intention can take the form of a thought or prayer that you want to focus on and develop through your attention and awareness. It can be a virtue or affirmation.

What you will no doubt discover is that the vibration of your meditation session will carry throughout your day. Your intentions will accompany you as you go about your daily routines and will help bring good results.

You will find your relationships improve because you are coming from a place of compassion. You will notice yourself being more mindful of others and the world around you, and you will probably not stumble or lose your keys quite as often. You may also find that doing your chores and necessary tasks is more pleasant and acceptable when done with a meditative frame of mind. On top of that, you will begin to feel a greater sense of joy as your spirit expands into awareness of the infinite realm of existence.

Singing while you wash your dishes can lift your spirit and make your task more pleasant. Humming along with the vacuum cleaner or clothes dryer adds a fun and musical element to ordinary chores and makes them much more enjoyable. As we learn to calm and focus our restless mind, we activate our greater consciousness and open up the channels of our intuition. In our daily lives, we will carry that still center point within us and we can solve our problems more easily. As we become more mindful, we have a greater awareness of our experiences, and are better able to take responsibility for our mental states as well as the physical condition of our lives.

CHAPTER 4

CONTROL THE BREATH, CONTROL THE MIND

How Do We Use Breath to Focus the Mind?

We can live without food and water for days or even weeks, but we cannot live without breath for more than a few minutes. Consider the importance of this for a moment as we honor the value and preciousness of the very air we breathe. The ancient yogis of India called it *prana* or Universal Energy. Some may call it the Life Force or the Holy Spirit, but whatever we call it, we know life depends on it. As we come to understand how to work with this universal energy, we learn that by controlling the breath we also control the mind.

The spiritual science of pranayama is about learning how to control the breath. In Sanskrit, the ancient language of India, the word *prana* means breath or energy and the word *yama* means control. By understanding how to control the breath/energy, we learn how to relax the body and control the subtle nuances of our minds. Obviously one of the best ways to calm the mind is through controlling the breath. The breath of life is a gift to treasure.

Typically we breathe using only a third of our lung capacity. This could mean we are living about 30% of our potential, shortening our years, and compromising our health. Often when we are anxious, angry, or afraid, we may find we are holding our breath. It is ironic that during these times of stress when we need to breathe deeply more than ever, we have cut off much of our oxygen supply. So now is a very good time to learn some helpful breathing techniques that will benefit us in our meditation as well as in our daily life.

Breath Exercises:

The following breath exercises can be done just a few times to get started. The breath counting is a step in the direction of breath awareness. It is not meditation, but it is a preparation for meditation and will be helpful in getting you to relax and understand the relationship between your breath and your mind. When you develop a comfort level with the breath counting, you may want to gradually increase the time of the exercise to five minutes or more. You may also want to begin your practice by clearing your lungs with a long exhalation and then proceed with whichever exercise or process you choose.

Breath Exercise 1
• Start by taking a full, deep inhalation through your nose.
• Fill your lungs completely.
• Then, exhale through your nose, slowly squeezing out every last bit of air.
• Repeat with a full inhalation followed by a long, slow exhalation.
• When complete, sit quietly and notice how you feel.

Breath Exercise 2
• Inhale through your nose as you count to 4.
• Hold breath in and count to 8.
• Exhale through your nose as you count to 8.
• Hold with breath exhaled and count to 8.
• Repeat several times.
• When comfortable, do breath counting for five minutes or more.
• When complete, sit quietly breathing fully in and out.

Breath Exercise 3
• Inhale deeply and fully through your nose.
• Exhale slowly through your mouth.
• Inhale again, hold a moment.
• Exhale slowly letting your voice make a small Ah sound, like a sigh.
• Repeat and continue to make a sighing sound as you exhale.
• When complete, enjoy the quiet sense of peace.

Breath Exercise 4

- Put your hand on your abdomen just below your navel.
- Notice the contraction and expansion of the diaphragm as you breathe.
- Take a few short panting breaths focusing on your exhalation so you can feel this muscle working.
- Exhale in short breaths through your mouth.
- Let there be a sound of Ha Ha Ha with the exhalation (like a laugh).
- Repeat several times.
- Experience the energy of your quiet mind.

Breath Exercise 5

- Breathe in deeply through your nose.
- Exhale slowly with your mouth closed making a humming sound.
- Repeat several times.
- Feel the vibration of the mmmm sound inside your head.
- When complete, notice the vibrations lingering within you.

Breath Exercise 6

- Inhale through your nose quickly.
- Hold for a moment.
- Exhale slowly through your mouth.
- Let your next exhalation be extended with the long sound of Haaaaaaaaa.
- Exhale completely, contracting the diaphragm muscle to squeeze all the air out.
- Repeat several times breathing in quickly and exhaling with long tone of Haaaaaaa.
- When complete, sit quietly and feel your energy circulating in your body.

Notice that when you add a sound to your exhalation, the breath naturally slows down. This is an example of 'toning' which we'll get to later. A basic rule of thumb with conscious breathing is to have a shorter inhalation and a much longer exhalation. This focus on the breath will help to slow down the parade of thoughts that is continually marching through your inner mind.

"Life is breathing light into every moment.

Take a deep breath and savor your field of

vibration filling the universe with love.

It feels so good to know there is no limit

to love lightening up the world and releasing

the constraints of our closed hearts."

—Dean Evenson

Breathing Meditation

Repeat to yourself either silently or out loud

I sit up straight with my spine erect but relaxed.

I take a deep breath, inhaling fully, holding for a
moment and then exhaling slowly and completely.

I feel the energy my breath brings
to every cell and molecule of my being.

Inhale. Hold. Exhale.

Exchanging energy.

Bringing in fresh, new, life-giving energy.

Letting go of what is old and used.

My breath is bringing in the life force.

I let go of what is unneeded. In and out.

With each breath, I am
restoring and revitalizing myself.

I am completely refreshed with each breath I take.

I am healthy. I am alive.

Mandala silkscreen by Dean Evenson

CHAPTER 5

SELF TALK, MONKEY MIND

Letting Go of Random Thoughts

"We are what we think.
All that we are arises with our thoughts.
With our thoughts we make the world.
Your worst enemy cannot harm you
As much as your own thoughts unguarded."

from Dhammapada, *The Sayings of the Buddha*,
translated by Thomas Byrom

When we're first beginning to meditate, we find that our minds are flooded with thoughts. Depending on our past experiences and current state of mind, these thoughts may be mundane and meaningless or fraught with worries and negativity. This mental activity is the typical state of the mind when it is not concentrating on something specific. The brain is a complex system of interconnected pathways and synapses that allow us to access memories and ideas which have been stored there from the beginning of our lives, and probably from even before we were born. The brain is constantly working, so when we decide to sit down and try to turn it off for a while in meditation, it is no wonder that this powerful organ does not immediately cooperate. It is just doing its job. Some have said that the mind is a wonderful servant but a terrible master.

Ideally, the mind should be serving the heart, the soul, and spirit of who we are. Unfortunately, when a mind is untrained, it can have a tendency to run rampant and try to tell us what to do based on its past programming. The basic nature of the mind is restlessness and transforming this restless mind is one of the goals of meditation.

With practice, the mind can be trained and then we can access its tremendous power and resources to serve us rather than to control us. The way we learn to let go of the barrage of random thoughts that the mind is constantly presenting is by using various techniques of concentration. The technique of focusing on breath awareness is just one of several that we can use to calm down our incessant thinking.

Focus and Concentration

Where Do We Focus Our Mind, Our Inner Eye, to Get the Most Benefit From Our Meditation Session?

There is a place behind our brow between our eyebrows that is called the third eye or spiritual eye. This area corresponds with our sixth chakra or mind and vision center, and is also known as the 'Christ Center' because it is the seat of our spiritual power. On a physical level, it is in the location of our pineal gland. When our eyes are closed, we want to have our inner gaze focusing inward just behind this spot. When our mind wanders, we always return our focus to our Spiritual Eye.

Even when our eyes are closed, they still tend to wander, following after an elusive thought. Instead of letting our attention follow that random thought, we bring our inner gaze to our single eye, our mind's eye. It is extraordinary how bringing our focus to this one spot can have such a profound effect in centering our awareness.

Consider the quote from the Bible:

> "The light of the body is the eye.
> If therefore thine eye be single,
> thy whole body shall be full of light."
> —Matthew 6:22, New Testament (KJV)

When we focus our concentration there on the Third Eye, everything in our mind and our body begins to shift. This place is a safe space to come back to, sort of like our spiritual home (and it's right there inside us 24/7).

Why Do We Need These Concentration Techniques?

Typically, we have a constant dialogue going on within our minds. We are continually telling ourselves something, and oftentimes it's not supportive. Picture a monkey sitting on your shoulder and whispering in your ears, nagging and cajoling you with irritating chatter. That's what is known as 'monkey mind.' The subject of this inner conversation can range anywhere from the news we heard on the radio to making a 'to do list,' or to replaying an unpleasant interaction with a friend, co-worker, or relative. Quite often, we are internally repeating something we were told about ourselves from a parent or ex-partner a long time ago. These kinds of repeated 'tape loops' can be very self-destructive. For instance, if our parent often said to us "Your room is a mess. You will never succeed" and we continue to replay this concept, we may find that we are internally re-affirming for ourselves that our life is a mess, and consequently success will continue to elude us.

It is very difficult to get these thought patterns out of our minds, and they especially tend to crop up when we are trying to meditate. This is why in meditation we use several concentration techniques to overcome the 'monkey mind,' and to help us let go of the destructive thoughts, and even the not-so-destructive thoughts that also interfere with the one-pointed concentration that is a goal of our meditation process. We already know that focusing on the breath can be a concentration device, and later we'll look into using mantra, chanting, and affirmations to help clear the mind of unnecessary clutter, thereby allowing us to enter a deeper state of inner quiet.

Finding Balance

As we contemplate this rising awakening of our spiritual awareness, we also remember to keep a balance between earth and sky, personal and community, material and spiritual. Therefore, it is important to remain grounded and feel our connection with the earth and the material realms. It's okay to have our head in the clouds as long as our feet are firmly on the ground. Meditation itself can help us to integrate the material and the spiritual realms because that's exactly what we are as human beings, a bridge between spirit and matter, a spirit with a body.

What we focus on expands.
Thought becomes speech.
Speech becomes action.
Action becomes manifestation.

Therefore, let us place our attention on thoughts and visions that are beautiful and good, life-affirming and supportive.

As we learn to control our mental processes, we find that we are able to create the kind of life we want. A maxim that began circulating in the '60s was "Go with the flow." Another was "You create your own reality." To some, there was a contradiction in these sayings leading to a confusion of principles. Dean and I, however, found them both to be true and have lived our lives to the fullest using them.

"Lighten up your load.
Let the dense thoughts float downstream
and loosen up the tight hold of thinking too much.
Let the light brighten your way to no thing, no time,
and no thought in a moment's notice."

—Dean Evenson

Go with the Flow.

Here's how it works as we understand it. We can't control everything in the world around us so sometimes things happen that we don't like and can't avoid (i.e., suffering, pain, sickness, loss, death). We can, however, choose how we respond to these things and navigate with less stress than if we mightily resisted them. So, when we are able to flow through a challenge, or move out of the way and let it flow around us (as in Tai Chi), we complete the karmic learning and move on.

Create Your Own Reality.

Now here's the other side of the story. In this aspect, we have our values, intentions, visions, and goals regarding how we want our lives to unfold, and we are constantly aiming in that direction. We make choices at every crossroads which move us toward our dreams and our goals. Things will continue to come up and we can still go with the flow to get through those challenges, but as we remain steadfast on the path, our lives improve. This is how we see it, and it has worked for us. You are welcome to give it a try!

CHAPTER 6
YOGA & TONING

The Purpose of Yoga as a Prelude to Meditation

Patanjali lived 2500 years ago in India, and is known for codifying the system of yoga. He wrote a series of Yoga Sutras in which he explained the fundamental aspects of yoga. Today, many people think of yoga as simply a physical exercise to keep the body in shape, but Patanjali explained it quite differently.

Yoga chitta vritti nirodha.
—Sutra 1.2 of Yoga Sutras of Patanjali

Here are some different translations of this sutra:

- Yoga is the stilling of the whirlpools of the mind.
- Yoga is the silencing of the modifications of the mind.
- Calm the waves and (re)unite the mind to its calm self.

The yoga stretches and postures were designed to help release energy from the physical body so that a person could sit in meditation for long periods of time without feeling restless. The true nature of yoga is to experience union – union with God, the soul, the Universe, whatever you want to call it. The word *yoga* itself means 'union' or 'yoke.'

By calming our mental whirlpools, we become capable of expanding our awareness to experience our oneness with the infinite. We may not experience this right away, but with practice, anything is possible.

Our goal in meditation is to focus on one thought, one mantra, one image, one breath at a time or whatever we choose to be our focus. By this singularity of focus, we find that the host of unregulated thoughts will drift away, and we will be able to access the depths of our inner being and tune into our higher consciousness.

In addition to breath awareness and focus, there are also a number of techniques related to using our voice, including toning, mantra, chanting, and affirmations, that we can use to enhance our focus.

Toning the Breath of Life

As we delve into the benefits of sound and breath in healing and meditation, we'll look more deeply into yoga, especially the concept of prana. The Sanskrit word *prana* has a depth of meanings: breath, breath of life, ancient, filled, old, full, life, power, air inhaled, vital organ, vital air, myrrh, respiration, spirit, vitality, energy, wind, spirit identified with the totality, dreaming spirits, poetical inspiration, vigor.

In our research, Dean and I were especially curious about the deeper meanings of prana as we were aware of its relationship with the breath. One day, we came across a movie about yoga called *Breath of the Gods* where we learned the story of a yogi named Krishnamacharya, who not only understood the subject of yoga, but was also a primary force in bringing yoga out of the caves and into modern life in the mid-20th century. From this film, we were surprised to learn that although the practice of yoga is over 5000 years old, it was virtually unknown in the late 1800s, even in India, except among a few dedicated souls living in caves and keeping the ancient yogic traditions alive. Krishnamacharya was going to change that. He studied and researched everything he could find about yoga, practiced relentlessly, and even spent seven years in a cave apprenticing with one of the last few yogis remaining. There he mastered over 3000 *asanas* (yoga postures) and developed many of his own. Over time, he evolved his own style of teaching, pioneering the sequencing of yoga postures and also prescribing therapeutic values to many of them.

Especially relevant to us was how he combined yoga postures (asanas) with intentional breathing (*pranayama*), thus making the asana practice part of the meditation itself, not just preparation for it. He taught that intentional breathing can have spiritual as well as physiological benefits. He also explained that this joint breathing and asana practice should be done in a spirit of devotion, and that practice done with this intention leads to inner calm.

Krishnamacharya instructed his students to close their eyes and concentrate on the point between the brows, and focus on a power greater than themselves, be it God, the sun, or nature. He spoke of the cycle of breath as an act of surrender. He said:

"Inhale, and God approaches you.
Hold the inhalation, and God remains with you.
Exhale, and you approach God.
Hold the exhalation, and surrender to God."

With this background in mind, we approach our modern day practice of meditation and yoga using many of the techniques originated by Krishnamacharya. During the four decades that Dean and I have practiced yoga and meditation, we have also explored the path of sound and music healing using vocal toning and breath work as part of our practice. As we mentioned, toning has the benefit of slowing down and elongating the exhalation by putting a brake on it. Slow down the breath and you slow down the heart rate. Slowing down the breath helps to slow down the incessant parade of thoughts crossing your mind.

We 'tone up' the body through exercise and muscle building. We can also 'tone up' the mind, and 'tune up' the spirit using our breath and voice to release tension. In the process, we can regain balance and equilibrium, and experience the peaceful Alpha or Theta brainwave states. Toning is an especially accessible way to do this because it doesn't require musical instruments or high tech equipment, just the human voice.

The beauty of toning is that it isn't about words or melodies; it is simply a neutral sound. You could begin with a simple vowel tone such as ahh or ohh. The longer one tones at a time, the greater the benefit will be in terms of relaxation of the whole body system and calming the mental processes.

That said, one could tone for 30 seconds or a few minutes and still feel a benefit. Through the breathing and toning process, we consciously invoke the life-giving energy of prana and enhance our own inner peace. We can use toning anytime to recharge ourselves throughout our workday. Additional benefit comes when we tone together as a couple or in a group, raising the vibrational energy, giving us a closer connection to each other, and enhancing the focus of our meditation.

What Is Vocal Toning?
How Do We Use Breath and Toning Together?

"In the beginning was the Word,
And the Word was with God,
And the Word was God."
—John1:1-2, New Testament (KJV)

In India, people believe that OM (or AUM) is the original sound of the universe and from that primal sound reverberated all existence.

Since we are becoming familiar with breathing techniques, let us look now at how we can use the breath to support a technique called 'vocal toning.' This system uses the vibration of the human voice to produce elongated vowel tones or humming sounds that can empower the meditation and at the same time balance the body systems. Toning also expands breathing ability and increases lung capacity.

In the process of toning, we use the breath to push out the voice in long sustained tones. The sound also acts like a 'brake' on the breath, helping to extend the exhalation. Toning is basically the sound of your vibrating breath, or the sound caused by your breath vibrating your vocal cords. Some people are not confident in their ability to sing or make sounds, but when a person simply focuses on just the breath, the tone follows naturally. No matter what level of experience a person has, toning can be a very satisfying experience.

Toning can be done alone or in groups, and there are advantages to both. Alone, you can exercise your voice and build your confidence. You can tone or sing in the shower, in the car, in the woods, or at the beach. When done in a group or with a partner, there can be an increased energy that occurs when people with a common intention tone together for a sustained period of time. This can be exhilarating and greatly enrich the meditation experience.

Humming is an especially gentle form of toning. The technique of humming can reach deeply into your body/being and can be done loudly or softly depending on your situation. You could even hum quietly under your breath at the supermarket and people probably won't notice. Allowing your breath to push out a sound can keep you focused and centered whether you are meditating or not.

Basic Toning Exercise:

A good way to begin toning is by taking a deep breath and exhaling as you let out a nice long Ahh sound, sort of like a long sigh. This is the vowel tone for the heart chakra. Along with each Ahh tone, you can imagine that you are sending out love, and with each inhalation, imagine you are receiving love. Do this several times and feel the resonance in your heart chakra.

OM/AUM

One of the most basic of sounds is OM. In Eastern traditions, this syllable is considered to be the seed of all sounds and is the foundation where we can begin our experience with toning. All else can follow the mighty OM. In Sanskrit, it is called a bija mantra. The word 'bija' means seed, and all other sounds grow from the bija or seed sounds. We concentrate on OM generated from our heart and solar plexus region and let it resonate deep into the center of our being. The long 'ohhh' at the beginning merges into the sustained sound of 'mmmm'. It sounds like A-U-M. The way you hold your mouth when pronouncing OM actually forms the letters A-U-M so both spellings are correct for the same basic sound.

Our good friend and chant singer, Deva Premal, explains this mantra metaphorically. She says the concept behind the OM mantra can be considered as three tones in one: A-U-M. The first AH tone is an opening up to love and a power greater than ourselves. The second tone of UH is more like a funnel drawing that energy into us. The third tone of MM resonates as a vibrant hum deep within us. By focusing on each sound separately as in A-U-M, we create a sacred cycle of breath and tone to enhance our well-being. With that in mind, you can tone the OM/AUM mantra and you will likely experience its deeper meaning and benefits.

HUM

HUM is another seed sound that resonates deeply within your being. It can also be toned under the breath like a soft humming resonating in your head. You can even do this softly in public places and not call attention to yourself. In Eastern cultures such as India, Nepal, and Tibet, people often chant mantras as they carry out their daily tasks.

Toning as a modern meditation technique has only come into public awareness during the past few decades although as an ancient rite it has appeared in many cultures and eras. With recent interest in sound healing, vocal toning has naturally emerged as a useful tool. Toning can be as simple and everyday as a sigh, a long vowel sound, or humming. Toning can also be as cosmic and sublime as a chakra tone or the sacred OM.

In a nutshell, vocal toning is simply letting out a long sound as you exhale. The breath is pushing the sound out and that long exhalation is slowing down the breath which in turn slows down the thoughts, quieting the mind, and helping the body to relax. It is an ideal sonic meditation tool.

We benefit greatly by incorporating toning into our meditation practice and using it along with other concentration techniques, including the third eye focus and mental breath awareness. By beginning with OM, we are invoking or inviting the universal presence into our being. From there, things can unfold accordingly. Doing an OM at the beginning and three OMs at the end of your practice can be a nice punctuation to your meditation experience.

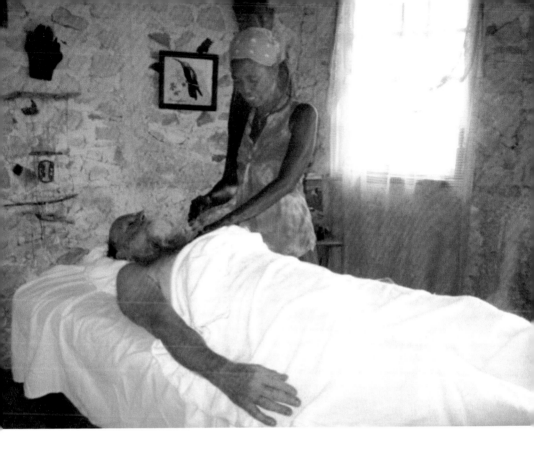

Toning for Therapists

Therapists can use toning in between client sessions to recharge and release stress and tension. If you are new to the idea of toning, we recommend starting slowly and picking a simple vowel tone like 'ah' or 'oh.' Inhale deeply and then slowly exhale as you gently express the sound with your breath. Repeat this multiple times for as long as you are comfortable. With regular practice and repetition, your voice will become strong and confident. When you find yourself between clients or meetings, you can take a few minutes to ground yourself using any toning practice that you have become familiar with. While toning, you can visualize that you are releasing any stored negative energy you may have picked up from your last client. Then you'll be renewed and ready for your next session.

NOTE: This clearing in the midst of a workday or stressful activity can be helpful in many life or work situations. Remember, also that using a low humming sound can be undetectable by others, and thus can even be done in public places.

Toning with Intention

Sound is a carrier wave for intention. When we tone OM or any other sound, we are sending out a vibration from our inner being to the ethers. If we connect the tone with an intention, affirmation, or a prayer, there can be an increased flow of blessing. Setting an intention prior to toning (and prior to your meditation for that matter) can be beneficial. It can be different each time, or the same. It's all up to you.

Years ago, we were privileged to host a group of Tibetan monks who were offering chant concerts and workshops across the country. We asked the chant master what made chanting useful in the healing and meditation process. He replied that the benefits come from the 'meaning' of the words and prayers that are being chanted. These monks were chanting scriptures that were sacred to them. We then realized that it wasn't just the sounds that were beneficial, but the intention behind the sounds that made them work. Then we asked him how the monks could make such amazing sounds with their voices. He replied "Practice. Three hours in the morning and three hours in the afternoon!" Well, that caught our attention. While we might not ever reach their levels of expertise, we can at least develop a regular practice of meditation, toning, and chanting. Our goal is to do a little more each day until we build up to the level we are striving for.

Remember, there are no hard or fast rules about toning or about meditation. There is only your experience. There are definitely guidelines and useful techniques that can help you along the way, but developing your own system or 'way' of meditation and toning will be the best. No one knows everything about meditation, the 'only way' or the best way to do it, so look around, listen, learn, and feel what resonates with your soul.

One nice thing about the uplifting and satisfying practice of toning is you can do it anywhere. It is even okay to do while driving. We would caution that many of the meditation techniques mentioned in this program should NOT be done in a car, but toning and chanting are actually good to do while driving as they keep you focused and centered. Always be your own judge about how you are able to stay grounded in situations where it is important to be aware of your physical environment.

"Letting go of all thought processes
is a quiet space available at any time.
Enhance the moment by letting go of all,
allowing the greater being to take care of
the details, and nurturing the result with
appreciation for the miracle of life."
—Dean Evenson

CHAPTER 7
PARTNER MEDITATION AND TONING

Spiritual Relationship

When two people have a spiritual practice in common, their relationship has a better chance of surviving and thriving. When they are able to sing, tone, chant, pray, or play instruments together, they can experience their connection in an even deeper way. Dean and I have been very fortunate to have both music and meditation happening in our relationship, and this certainly keeps more fun in the equation. We have grown in our spiritual journeys, both individually and as a couple, and we are grateful for the spiritual practice that we share because we know how much it has helped our relationship to flourish. We hope others will consider a shared path using music and sound to enhance their spiritual connection.

For many years, Dean and I taught workshops on meditation and sound healing. In the process, we got a lot of practice toning in groups and appreciated every minute of it. Eventually though, we discovered that by applying those toning practices in our personal life, we especially benefitted from toning together just as a couple. Through the years, we have spent many long, comfortable evenings toning together as we lay amongst the pillows on our comfy couch. We might start off with a low hum and let it grow, flow, and change as we enjoy the simple process of breathing and vibrating together. We feel very comfortable toning together probably because we do it so often. So, we suggest that if you want to enhance intimacy with your partner or good friend, try toning together on a regular basis.

Sometimes, Dean and I tone in the car and it centers us. Other times, we sing along with our favorite kirtan or chant music. There are many ways to join together in musical meditations, and I'm sure new ways are being invented every day by couples across the globe. To be clear about the concept of intimacy, it does not apply to just sexual, sensual, or adult relationships. Intimacy applies as well to a mother and child, brother and sister, and friends. Children can have fun with the toning experience too.

Simply taking time to sit together in a quiet space without talking can improve the partner bond. There is a whole system of partner meditation in the Hindu tradition called Tantra which in some aspects involves sexuality. This is not to be confused with the Tantra practice of Tibetan Buddhists which does not have to do with partners or sexuality (as far as we know). We will be addressing partner meditation here in a non-sexual way with activities that can be done by couples or by friends and fellow practitioners.

Conscious toning can release tensions and bring a sense of exhilaration and feeling of 'aliveness.' It can help to balance or tune up the whole body system. When toning with another person, listening is a major component as it involves blending one's own voice with another's voice. In addition, finding the space between the breaths allows access to a meditative state of quiet stillness.

Partner toning isn't for everyone, so even if your significant other isn't interested, you may want to consider toning with a friend. There is great benefit as two or more people feel comfortable breathing together and sounding resonant tones. When people allow themselves to open to this sort of intimate sound connection, magic occurs creating a deeper sense of familiarity.

In partner meditation, you can sit face-to-face, side-by-side, back-to -back, or even lying down next to each other. Each has its advantages, so experiment and choose what works best for you.

10 Simple Steps to a More Intimate Relationship Through Vocal Toning:

1. Find a place to sit together, across from or next to your friend.

2. Take a deep breath, hold a moment and release.

3. As you exhale, allow a quiet humming to occur as you push the breath out.

4. Do this several times until your hum resonates with your partner's hum.

5. Inhale again and slowly exhale pushing out a vowel tone with the breath.

6. Begin with AH or OH. Repeat slowly and continue as many times as you want.

7. Play with the sound. Listen to the other. Change the vowel tone.

8. Tone the chakras. Tone the refrigerator. They both hum!

9. Tone the depths of the earth. Tone the high celestial heavens.

10. Feel the vibration of oneness. Breathe into each other's soul.

Partner Meditation Exercises:

1. Sit face-to face with your knees touching.

   Let one of your hands face up and in contact
   with your partner's downward facing hand.

   Your other hand will be facing down and in contact with
   your partner's upturned hand.

   Don't grasp the hands but simply feel a light touch
   and sense energy flowing between your hands.

   An alternative is for both of you to sit
   with your hands in your own lap or resting on your knees.

   Do whatever suits you.

2. As you face each other, gaze into each other eyes.

   You can also adjust your gaze with your eyes relaxed and
   slightly out of focus so you see three eyes with one right
   in the middle of your partner's forehead.

   This takes some practice but it is a helpful form of
   meditation where you are not focusing your eyes, but
   focusing on your inner eye.

3. When you settle into a peaceful state with your partner, you
   may want to close your eyes and bring your attention to your
   energy body, feeling it extend out to touch your partner's
   energy body.

   Rest in the peacefulness of that connection.

4. As you face each other, place your right hand on your partner's heart.

   Focus on your breath as you tune first into the physical heart, and then into the emotional energy of the heart.

   Take a deep breath together and exhale with the sound of AH, extending it as long as possible.

   AH is the sound of the heart chakra, so focus on giving and receiving unconditional love with your partner.

   Repeat this as many times as you feel comfortable.

   When complete, let your hands drop down in your lap and become silent. Focus on your breathing and feel the gentleness of the love between you.

5. Another option is to sit back-to-back with your spines touching and hands gently resting on your knees.

   Listen for the sound of the each other's breathing and let your breath begin to synchronize.

   Begin to tone with a low humming.

   Feel your partner's body vibrating with the hum.
   Let the hum grow louder.

   Continue this for as long as comfortable.

6. When you are complete with your meditation, you might try this simple closing ritual.

   Face each other, sitting or standing, and make a small bow, with hands together as in a prayer position and say "Thank you."

   Or you may bow and say, "Namasté," a Sanskrit word that means "I honor the light within you." It is often said at the ending of a meditation, and it also serves as both a greeting and farewell.

   Closing with a hug is also appropriate.

   Needless to say, there are no set rules for partner meditation or meditation in general, so go with what feels good and comfortable to you both.

Chakra artwork by our son, Elijah Evenson

CHAPTER 8
SOUNDING THE CHAKRAS

Overview of the Chakras

Now let's look into the relationship between toning and the mysterious orbs called chakras. We love this field of study because it explains a lot about how we function as human beings. When we understand and optimize our energy centers (i.e., chakras), we allow the unity of our whole being to function at its highest capacity. Awareness of the chakras is extremely beneficial in helping balance the whole body/mind system.

As it turns out, breath, toning, and affirmations can play a big part in activating the chakras while at the same time helping to deepen our meditative experience. In this next section, we give a simple overview of the chakras and explain how to use toning to invigorate the chakras and thereby balance out whatever bodily, emotional, mental or spiritual aspects of our being need attention.

In Sanskrit, the word *chakra* means 'a wheel that spins.' We can imagine them as orbs or spherical balls of vibrational energy. The concept of chakras originated in the ancient wisdom traditions of India and their mention appears as far back as 1500-500 BC in sacred Vedic and Upanishad texts. The chakras also appear in the Yoga Sutras of Patanjali. Today, people are rediscovering the meaning of the chakras and finding modern applications to assist in their meditation and healing practices.

To visualize the chakras, picture seven interconnected spheres or balls of energy stacked on top of each other, beginning at the base of the spine and continuing up along the body's central meridian to the crown of the head. Each of these energy vortices is associated with different major organs and glandular systems, but the chakras are not limited to just the functioning of the material body. You might consider them as doorways between the physical and subtle aspects of our being. As such, they have psychological, emotional, mental, and spiritual functions, and they are essential to the harmonious integration of the whole being. Understanding the chakra system can assist in helping us go beyond seeing ourselves as mere physical beings and allow us to connect with the more spiritual and emotional parts of our being.

The first three lower chakras are related to the physical characteristics of our being and are associated with the elements of Earth, Water, and Fire. These chakras relate to our survival needs for food, water, and energy. The first chakra, located at the base of the spine, has to do with our foundation, our sense of support and grounding, and it relates to the Earth element. The second chakra is related to our passion, creativity, and relationships. It involves flow and the Water element. The third chakra, in the abdominal area, is our power center, the engine of our being, and it relates to the element of Fire as in the concept of 'fire in the belly.'

Our fourth chakra, or heart chakra, is the nexus of transition between the three lower physical chakras and the three higher spiritual chakras. This chakra relates to the element Air and is about exchanging energy. This is reflected in our breathing process where we breathe in oxygen and exhale carbon dioxide. It so happens that plants breathe in carbon dioxide and exhale oxygen. What a perfect example of giving and receiving. Of course, this chakra involves Love in its many facets, giving and receiving unconditional love for all and especially for oneself.

The top three chakras relate to our more spiritual centers. The fifth chakra, at the throat level, has to do with communication, relating to the element of Sound or Ether. The sixth chakra is our mental center and relates to Vision and Light. Our seventh chakra, at the top of our head, is our crown chakra and connects us with consciousness and Spirit.

A helpful method for bringing the chakras into balance utilizes the voice to tone and resonate the chakras, helping to strengthen and empower them. Since sound is a subtle energy, it has the ability to alter our state of consciousness. When sound is coupled with focus and intention, the result is magnified, and by using the breath to push out the tones, coupled with focusing our attention on our chakras, we increase the benefit of our meditation.

NOTE: There are several systems related to understanding and toning with the chakras. Some are ancient and some have been adapted to modern use. We believe there is no right or wrong or 'only' way, so we encourage you to try out the various systems and determine which one resonates with you and start there. You can even modify the practice to suit your own temperament and needs. This concept goes with everything discussed here. If it works for you, use it. If not, feel free to ignore.

Bija Mantras

Here is an ancient practice of toning with the chakras that originates in traditions of India. As we mentioned before, in the Sanskrit language, the word for seed is *bija* and thus these sounds are called seed sounds or bija mantras. These sounds are often intoned in a monotone, without moving up or down a scale, and have a long 'mmm' at the end.

Here they are in order from first to seventh chakra:

LAM, VAM, RAM, YAM, HAM, SHAM, AUM

Bija Mantra Toning Exercise:

Tone in a monotone from root to crown.

Inhale, and as you exhale, intone:

- *Lam*
- *Vam*
- *Ram*
- *Yam*
- *Ham*
- *Sham*
- *A-U-M*

Repeat this exercise multiple times.

Bija Mantra Toning Exercise with One Tone per Breath:

- Take a deep breath in and focus on the first chakra.

- As you breathe out, tone Lam for the full exhalation.

- Inhale again and do the same with each additional bija mantra.

- Focus on the relevant chakra.

- When complete, sit quietly and feel the energy in your body.

Bija Mantra Toning Exercise Raising Arms:

- To enhance the effectiveness, start with your arms in your lap and gradually raise them as you chant all the bija mantras in a monotone.

- When you reach the top and have finished toning AUM, let the arms circle around and come back to the lap.

- Then take another deep breath and repeat the cycle.

- Do this multiple times, and when complete, sit quietly and let the energy resonate with your chakras.

NOTE: About bija mantras—There are several systems of toning the bija mantras. We have chosen the system taught by Deepak Chopra. Another system is to use OM for the Sixth Chakra instead of Sham. In that case, the Seventh Chakra is silent. Please use whichever system resonates with you.

Vowel Toning

Another way of sounding the chakras is through singing simple vowel tones. A system we learned from our friend and fellow musician, Jonathan Goldman, uses specific vowel tones for each of the seven chakras.

These vowel sounds can be intoned in a scale, beginning with the Root chakra at the base, and ascending to the Crown chakra at the peak. This ascent is accompanied by the seven vowels:

UH, OO, OH, AH, EYE, AYE, EEE.

These open vowel tones can be extended a long time. Color visualizations and affirmations can be integrated as well as well (see 'Key to the Chakras' chart).

Vowel Toning Exercise
One Breath Per Each Chakra:

- Take a deep breath and, as you exhale,
  tone *UH* until you have exhaled completely.
- Take another deep breath and as you exhale,
  tone *OO* at a slightly higher pitch.
- Continue up the scale, raising the pitch
  with each successive chakra tone.

Vowel Toning Exercise
All Chakras On One Breath:

- Take a very deep breath
  and in the space of a single exhalation, intone
  UH, OO, OH, AH, EYE, AYE, EEE
  each at a slightly higher pitch.
- Then tone from top to bottom if you like.
- Try both ways and use whichever suits you best.

Hindustani Scale

Yet another system of toning the chakras is similar to the basic solfège musical scale that many of us in the West are familiar with of *Do Re Mi Fa Sol La Ti Do*. It is called the Hindustani scale and also originates in India. Because we are accustomed to completing an octave once we have started, the scale includes an 8th note.

Here is the Hindustani scale from Root to Crown:

SA RE GA MA PA DHA NI (SA)

So if *SA* were the root note C, then *RE* would be D, etc. This is a fulfilling way to relate to the chakras and for some reason we find it more powerful using these sounds rather than the familiar solfège.

Hindustani Scale Exercises: Root Note C

- *SA*   (C) low
- *RE*   (D)
- *GA*   (E)
- *MA*   (F)
- *PA*   (G)
- *DHA* (A)
- *NI*   (B)
- *SA*   (C) the octave high

Hindustani Exercises:

1. Take a deep breath and tone *SA* on the exhalation emptying your lungs completely.
2. Breathe in and tone the next note *RE*.
3. Repeat with each note up the scale.
4. Then try doing the whole scale on one breath.
5. Repeat this several times.
6. Once you are familiar with the notes, reverse the scale starting with the high C and descending to the low C (or whatever note you choose as your root note).

Chakra Affirmations

Another way of using sound and breath to resonate the chakras is to use a short affirmation to sing or state what one wants to focus on for each chakra. It is important that the statement is positive and in the present tense. Repeating your affirmations frequently with high intention, and/or using the toning and color visualizations can help to create healthy chakras that will support the well-being of body, mind, and spirit.

To keep all this from being too confusing, we have put a simple chart together to remind you of the various tones from each of the systems along with a color associated with the chakra, and a short affirmation that reflects the essence of the chakra. Please don't let it overwhelm you. Remember, these are just tools and it is important that they resonate for you. Use the list to help you get the overall picture, try each system out, and then pick one of them to experiment with until you find what works for you.

7th Chakra I am one with the infinite all, my higher self, angelic guidance.

6th Chakra My mind is clear and open to divine wisdom.

5th Chakra I speak my truth clearly and kindly.

4th Chakra I give and receive unconditional love.

3rd Chakra I am one with the power of the universe.

2nd Chakra I am creative and connected.

1st Chakra I am grounded and supported.

KEY TO THE CHAKRAS

The following is a key to the organs, functions, tones, and affirmations of each Chakra:

#	NAME	COLOR	ELEMENT	HINDUSTANI SCALE	BIJA MANTRA	VOWEL TONE		AFFIRMATION
7	CROWN	Violet	Spirit	NI	Aum	EEE		*I am one with the infinite all, my higher self, angelic guidance*
	Sanskrit Name: Sahasrara. Spirit, consciousness, oneness. Brain, nerves, cerebral cortex, pituitary gland.							
6	THIRD EYE	Indigo	Light	DHA	Sham	AYE		*My mind is clear and open to divine wisdom*
	Sanskrit Name: Ajna. Insight, intuition, vision. Brow, eyes, pineal gland.							
5	THROAT	Blue	Sound	PA	Ham	EYE		*I speak my truth clearly and kindly*
	Sanskrit Name: Vissudha. Communication, identity, clarity. Mouth, vocal cords, ears, thyroid gland.							
4	HEART	Green	Air	MA	Yam	AHH		*I give and receive unconditional love*
	Sanskrit Name: Anahata. Love, compassion, giving-receiving. Cardiac plexus, heart, lungs, thymus gland.							
3	SOLAR PLEXUS	Yellow	Fire	GA	Ram	OHH		*I am one with the power of the universe*
	Sanskrit Name: Manipura. Personal power, will power, action. Stomach, liver, kidneys, pancreas, digestion, adrenals.							
2	SACRAL	Orange	Water	RE	Vam	OOO		*I am creative and connected*
	Sanskrit Name: Svadhisthana. Emotions, relationships, creativity. Reproductive system, bladder, intestines, hips.							
1	ROOT	Red	Earth	SA	Lam	UHH		*I am grounded and supported*
	Sanskrit Name: Muladhara. Self-preservation, security, survival. Base of spine, coccygeal plexus, rectum, perineum.							

This image is of the Sanskrit mantra
OM MANI PADME HUM
transliterated into Tibetan script.

CHAPTER 9
PERSONAL EMPOWERMENT THROUGH MANTRA

Monkey Mind or Clear Mind? Why Does Mantra Mean Mind Protection?

We need to place a guardian at the gate of our awareness to keep the demons of our mental processes from distracting us, and mantra is one way to do this. The word *mantra* means 'mind protection' in Sanskrit. A mantra is a short sacred sound or phrase, usually with spiritual significance. A mantra carries a vibration and frequency that extends beyond the simple meaning of its words. In the highest sense, mantras carry thought waves that can energize the prana through constant repetition and they can reach deep into the subconscious mind to access the collective consciousness. More simply, using mantra can help overcome mental chatter, and prepare the way for an expansion of consciousness.

Mantra Yoga

There are many forms of yoga, each dealing with different aspects of our being. For instance, hatha yoga involves physical postures or asanas. Kundalini yoga works with the breath through pranayama. Bhakti yoga has to do with devotion. Dharma yoga expresses itself by being of service. And mantra yoga involves the centering the consciousness within through japa—the repetition of certain universal root words/sounds representing a particular aspect of Spirit.

Mantras can be in Sanskrit, English, Hebrew, Latin, or other languages. They can be ancient and passed on from guru (teacher) to devotee (student). In cases like that, they may have a strong connection with a long spiritual tradition. They can also be created by an individual based on their personal values, needs, or issues. Typically, mantras are statements of profound spiritual truth that resonate with the person repeating them. They may also be short affirmations that are easily repeated. In fact, it is in the repetition of a mantra that power lies.

I AM

A mantra that many people might relate with is simply I AM. One way to use it is to say 'I' as you are breathing in, and to say 'AM' as you are breathing out. You may like to expand it to say 'I am – alive' or 'I am – love' and it will have a similar beneficial effect. Affirming simple, basic truths can help to clear the judgments and ego attachments that normally clutter our thoughts, thereby opening us up to a greater sense of inner peace. So, whether you are using an ancient mantra or a personal one that you create, we hope you will try using mantra to empower your soul and spirit, and to become your highest self.

SO HAM

SO HAM (sometimes spelled 'SO HUM') is called the natural mantra because it follows the natural sound of the in and out breath. You inhale SO, and exhale HAM. SO means 'That' and HAM means 'I'. Thus, the mantra means 'I AM THAT.' The inhalation of SO is an inward sucking sound. It might feel funny at first, but with practice it can work.

OM TARE TUTARE TURE SVAHA

This is another very special mantra that we learned from His Holiness the Dalai Lama at a workshop on Patience many years ago. It is called the *Green Tara Mantra*.

This mantra is an invocation of Tara who, according to the Tibetan world view is a mother goddess of compassion similar to Quan Yin, Mother Mary, or even Mother Earth. She is the ultimate mother you can call on in times of need.

TUTARE means swift action and TURE means to dispel sickness and misery. So, we invoke the Universal Oneness and invite Tara to come swiftly into our lives to dispel any sickness or negativity that might exist. SVAHA (also pronounced Swaha or Soha) is a concluding declaration, somewhat like *Amen* or *So be it!*

OM MANI PADME HUM

In the toning section, we talked about OM (AUM) which is a most basic and powerful mantra. It can be chanted alone or as part of another mantra. A familiar mantra used by millions of people worldwide is the six-syllable mantra, OM MANI PADME HUM. This is a good mantra to begin using because it carries a lot of power due to the daily repetition by very many people from ancient times until today. When translated literally, it means Homage or Praise to the Jewel in the Lotus Indivisible.

OM invokes the universal seed sound of all sounds, the spirit of creation, of universal oneness. MANI is the jewel, which stands for the highest principles, the method, or way to enlightenment. PADME is the lotus of wisdom which grows into great beauty from the mud of material existence. HUM designates their union and indivisibility. This is a very simplified explanation of a complex concept, and it really isn't that important to know the underlying meaning because the mantra carries a power that transcends language. Dean and I use this mantra a lot as it is easy to say and it is quite effective.

Repeat a Mantra and Focus on Your Breathing.

Mantra Practice 1: I AM, I AM, I AM

Mantra Practice 2: OM MANI PADME HUM

Mantra Practice 3: OM TARE TUTARE TURE SVAHA

Mantra Practice 4: SO HAM, SO HAM, SO HAM

CHAPTER 10
MY SELF-HEALING THROUGH SINGING

How I Used Mantra to Heal

Many years ago, I was dealing with some health issues. I had hearing loss in my right ear, and I was having bouts of dizziness and nausea that were very debilitating. These episodes went on for a year or so. I did all the medical diagnostics, yet no one could tell me what was wrong. I was under a lot of stress at the time, but with no medical answers, I realized I had to figure it out for myself. I slowed down my work schedule and improved my diet, but nothing seemed to alleviate my symptoms. In the process of trying to figure out my situation, I read a couple of books on the power of the mind and its role in making us sick or making us well. I knew there was something going on in my mind that was contributing to my ailments. Another thing I did was to sign up for several toning workshops offered by sound healing pioneer, Don Campbell. I thought working on my hearing issue from the inside might help, and I knew that toning created vibrations in the head itself so perhaps it could vibrate my hearing back.

One of the books I read asked the questions, "Are you singing every day? Are you feeling joy?" Pondering these questions, I realized that I was too busy worrying about my business, and trying to fix everything. On top of that, I was swamped with a slew of self-deprecating thoughts. Something had to change. I decided to create a mantra for myself that dealt with my own issues. For many years, Dean and I had been using the *Green Tara Mantra* we had learned from the Dalai Lama, and we had really appreciated its centering effects. But now I needed something in English that spoke to my issues. I needed to clear the cobwebs of self-judgment and worry from my mind. I wanted to open my heart to love and let go of judgments about myself and others. In essence, I wanted to feel well again. In fact, I wanted the whole world to feel well!

The mantra I came up with was this:

"Clear my mind. Open my heart. Heal my body. Heal my world."

I added a little melody to it and would sing it as often as possible. I went for walks in the woods while singing it. I also praised the trees, the birds, the air, and even the people I passed along the trail. After singing my mantra for a week to ten days, I noticed that my dizzy spells had gone away and not returned. In fact, they were completely vanquished after nearly a year of tormenting me. A few months later, I noticed that my hearing was starting to improve and now years later my hearing is still much improved. To me it was a miracle, and I attribute my healing to singing my mantra!

This sort of mantra is like a 'spiritual jingle,' the kind you wouldn't mind replaying over and over in your mind because its message is for the purpose of healing. If we can heal ourselves, then it is only natural that we can also heal our relationships and the world around us. This was my personal prayer, and I knew I had to begin with my own priority project – my mind!

How Do We Create a Personal Mantra?

You can also create a personal mantra that speaks to your soul and sings to your heart. It can be a prayer, an affirmation, a simple song, or just two or three words. It can affirm what you want to empower in your life. It can invoke the support that you want on your journey. If you want more peace in your life, you could say "I am peace." If you want more love in your life, you could say "I give and receive love" or "Love flows to me and through me." Remember to keep it short and sweet and easy to repeat. It should also be positive and in the present tense.

Personal Mantra Practices

- Personal Mantra Practice 1:
  Clear my mind. Open my heart. Heal my body. Heal my world.

- Personal Mantra Practice 2:
  Create a short personal mantra and repeat it often.

  NOTE TO READER: If you are dealing with a serious medical issue, please consult a physician. Using mantra and affirmations can be helpful but they should not be used in place of or instead of proper medical care.

"Watch your thoughts,
for they become words.
Choose your words,
for they become actions.
Understand your actions,
for they become habits.
Study your habits, for they
will become your character.
Develop your character, for
it becomes your destiny."
—Anonymous

CHAPTER 11

HOW TO USE POSITIVE AFFIRMATIONS TO CREATE THE LIFE YOU DESIRE

What Are Affirmations?

Do you ever feel anxious as you try to digest the constant barrage of news hitting you? Bad news affects all of us, painting a pessimistic picture of the world, coloring the content of our thoughts. How do we overcome tendencies toward worry, negativity, or just simply too much thinking? How can we harness the power of positive energy to improve our lives and manifest our dreams? Understanding how affirmations work may hold a key.

An affirmation is a positive statement asserting that a desired goal is already achieved. It is a declaration to manifest a desired outcome although this desired way of being may seem far from the truth at the moment. However, in a truly amazing way, with enough repetition and focused intention, declaration can become reality. Since the subconscious mind processes affirmations and suggestions as reality, it is important to be aware of one's thoughts and to constantly edit out unwanted negative suggestions.

The fact is, we are constantly affirming in our mind what we believe. When we look honestly at the content of our thoughts, we may be shocked to realize what we have been telling ourselves on a regular basis. We can usually tell the quality of our subconscious mind by looking at the quality of our life. If we are not pleased with our life, we might wish to look at the content of our mind to discover how we have been programming our existence to coincide with our belief structure.

In the 1950s, Earl Nightingale, cofounder of Nightingale-Conant personal development company, recorded a classic motivational record called *The Strangest Secret*. He identified the "strangest secret" as this: We become what we think about every day. He emphasized the power of positive self-talk, expectation, and belief. These ideas were ground breaking at the time, but today, many people use guided affirmations in some way in service of achieving their goals. Like any other tool of transformation, skill and understanding are required to actualize their potential.

Why Do Affirmations Work?
What Makes Them So Effective?

When we take hold of our thoughts through the repetition of positive affirmations, we can move in the direction of manifesting our highest ideals and vision for our lives.

Through the use of a repeated phrase, prayer, or affirmation, we can overcome the rampant thoughts and tape loops that tend to guide our behavior. By repeating a phrase over and over again, it becomes embedded in our subconscious mind, and then the creative forces of the universe rally support in order to make it happen. Repetition increases the effectiveness of affirmations. In the negative aspect of this principle, we experience inner 'tape loops' that constantly replay a phrase or thought that is not in our best interests. This thought may be something a parent or ex-partner told us about ourselves long ago like "You are a mess" or "You'll never amount to anything." We may have unconsciously repeated this idea for years, creating a messy, unfulfilling life for ourselves in the process.

Affirmations only work when spoken in the present tense. The subconscious mind takes things very literally, so if you say "I will be rich," you probably will not experience prosperity in the present moment. It will always be just around the corner, in the elusive future.

Speaking affirmations out loud energizes them. Speaking them repeatedly creates habituation. Though the actual statement may be different from our current circumstance, when we put our feelings into the words, we come closer to experiencing the fulfillment of our desires. For affirmations to truly work, they require belief and faith in them, even though the actual statement may be different from our current circumstance. We increase their effectiveness when we put our feelings into them and actually experience the emotions connected with the fulfillment of our desires.

When we take hold of our thoughts and use affirmations regularly with an understanding of how they work, positive change will occur. When we can clearly visualize and feel the reality of the spoken word affirmation, we enter into a cooperative contract with the universe, making use of this powerful tool to manifest our highest dreams.

With perseverance, repetition, and our steadfast belief in them, the words of our affirmations become a part of us. Before long, we look around and realize we are actually achieving what we may have thought was impossible only weeks or months before.

Affirmation Principles:

1. Positive Phrase
2. Present Tense
3. Spoken Aloud or Silently
4. Repetition and Habituation
5. Belief and Faith
6. Feelings and Emotions

Repeat the Following Affirmations
Silently or Aloud as Many Times as You Like:

• **Affirmation Exercise 1** - *Attraction:*

I am a magnet for all that is good in the world.
I attract what I want and I'm filled with life's blessings.
I focus on love and attract love into my life.
I focus on joy and a sense of joy fills me with its presence.
I focus on creating a perfect life for myself
and for those around me and that is exactly what happens.

• **Affirmation Exercise 2** - *Releasing:*

I release and let go of that which no longer serves me.
I easily and freely release and let go of thoughts,
feelings, and attachments that are not helpful
to my being the very best person I can be.
I let go of anything that is holding me back
from fulfilling my life's purpose.
I am free.

- **Affirmation Exercise 3 -** *Focus:*

  I realize that what I focus on expands.
  I therefore choose to focus on what
  is good and beautiful in my world.
  I focus with gratitude on what I have in life
  rather than on what might be lacking.
  In the process of acceptance,
  many blessings come my way.
  I find my own center by
  focusing on the spirit within.

- Affirmation Exercise 4 - *Personal Affirmation:*

  Create your own short affirmation
  and use it daily. Notice how it changes
  your life view and experience.

Gina Salá and Deobrat Mishra performing kirtan

CHAPTER 12
HOW ARE CHANT, PRAYER, MANTRA, AND KIRTAN DIFFERENT?

Chant

Chant involves singing or reciting a phrase or mantra. It can be done alone or in a group, aloud or in silence. The word *chant* comes from a root 'chanter' which means 'to sing' in French or 'cantare' in Latin. A common form of chant is simply chanting the names of God/Goddess over and over again. Through rhythmic repetitive singing of sacred words, sacred mantras, sacred songs, or ancient sounds, one is able to enter a deep spiritual space. Many cultures and religions from ancient times to this day have used chant as a way to elevate one from the physical aspects of the daily world to a higher place.

Prayer

Prayer is a specific act of addressing God or a deity as a form of worship or petition. Prayers can be of praise and honor, specific requests for assistance, confession, or general request for divine guidance. Also, there are prayers of gratitude which are always appropriate because when we are grateful for what we already have, we can open the way for receiving what we truly want. Prayer tends to involve actively speaking to God, whereas meditation is more an act of inner listening. Setting one's intention before meditating can be a form of prayer or invocation.

Daniel Paul on tablas, and Gina Salá chanting with harmonium

Deobrat Mishra sitar and Dean Evenson flute

Mantra

Mantra is a sacred word, phrase, or short affirmation that is repeated over and over again. Through repetition, one sets up a resonant field that creates a vibration of sacred stillness. By focusing on one mantra or phrase, we are able to dispel the rampant thoughts that constantly disturb our minds.

Kirtan

Kirtan is a form of devotional singing, using a call and response format that is usually done in groups with a leader and followers. It can be a very enlivening and enriching experience. In Sanskrit, the word *kirtan* means 'repeat.' Thus, the followers repeat the chant of the leader. Through this participatory singing experience, one can benefit greatly from the group energy. Kirtan can definitely help the mind to become quiet, even as the chants of the group may become louder, more dynamic, or even ecstatic.

Each of these forms—chant, prayer, mantra, and kirtan—when practiced with authentic intention, can greatly benefit anyone and everyone who participates in them.

CHAPTER 13

USE OF PRAYER BEADS AND SINGING BOWLS

How to Use Mala, Rosary, or Prayer Beads

Another helpful tool in the chanting of mantra or saying affirmations is prayer beads that can be used to count the recitations.

Many cultures and religions have used beads to help maintain a focus on their prayers. Catholics use a rosary to repeat their 'Hail Mary' prayer. Hindus use beads to count their mantra. Tibetans use a mala or prayer beads to stay focused on the mantra.

The strings of beads in the East often have 108 beads. With each repetition of the mantra, one uses the thumb and first finger to move from one bead to the next. The goal certainly isn't just to count the prayers, but it does help one to stay focused on the chant and keep moving on without becoming distracted by random thoughts.

People also use mantra as they go about their day to help them stay connected with their center. The goal of meditation is not just to have a nice experience for a few minutes or an hour but rather to carry the energy of that experience throughout your day. Perhaps by carrying a string of prayer beads around, you can use it to count your prayers, taking advantage of time normally spent waiting in line or doing another activity that doesn't require your focus.

Mantra Counting:

- Use beads to count your prayers 108 times or however many times you want to.

How to Use Tibetan Bowls and Bells

Tibetan singing bowls are an ancient tool used to assist in the meditation process. The origin of Tibetan bowls is shrouded in mystery, but it is certain that monks used them as an aid in their meditation practice. Ancient bowls were made of an alloy composed of as many as twelve different metals that were pounded and shaped into bowls.

When a wooden mallet strikes a bowl, a rich blend of harmonic overtones is created. Because of the multiple harmonics, the sound can have the effect of bringing both hemispheres of the brain into synchronization. One can also use the wooden mallet to rub the edge of the bowl and create a pleasing tone. By focusing on the sound of the bowl tone as it lingers, one can experience a sort of transcendent state. By slowly playing several bowls, bells, or cymbals, the experience can be expanded. Some people may prefer to use crystal bowls of varying sizes instead. Both can have a beneficial effect.

Whether used in meditation or simply to create a calm, serene state, the clear tones of the bowls can evoke a sense of harmony and balance. In this way, sound can be the medium that transports a person to an elevated state of consciousness.

Singing Bowl Exercises

- Singing Bowl Exercise 1:
  Strike a bowl and listen to the sound resonate until silence.

- Singing Bowl Exercise 2:
  Then strike another bowl and do the same.

- Singing Bowl Exercise 3:
  Breathe in and as you exhale, try to tone
  with the lingering tone of the bowl.

- Singing Bowl Exercise 4:
  Strike a second bowl before the first sound stops
  and focus on their resonance.

CHAPTER 14
HOW IS A WALKING MEDITATION DIFFERENT FROM SITTING?

We usually think that meditation is done sitting, but it can also be beneficial to practice walking meditation. In this case, walking with the eyes open, one is more mindful of the outside world. The purpose of a walking meditation is to cultivate awareness, and to use the very act of walking as a focus of your concentration thereby allowing you to have a wakeful presence. Once mastered, this wakeful presence can be carried over into more active and engaged parts of your life, allowing you to be calm and peaceful in any situation. In the Bible, Jesus expressed an aspect of this concept as being "in the world but not of it."

There are several ways to include walking as part of your meditation practice. All these ways encourage keeping a focus on the breath, and music can also be involved. Walking in silence is good in and of itself, but if you choose to add a musical element, you may wish to use headphones and listen to meditative music as you walk mindfully. Another way to use music is to chant a mantra, say an affirmation, or sing a prayerful song as you walk. Any of these will help you to stay focused and centered, and to get more out of the experience.

Simple Walking Meditation Techniques

A simple walking meditation technique is to walk in a small designated area, either inside or outdoors. You can walk back and forth from one point to another, or you can choose to walk in a circle. Begin by standing tall with your eyes closed and with your arms resting comfortably at your sides. Feel the ground beneath your feet and notice the environment. Take a few deep breaths then open your eyes. As you take a step forward, notice the shifting from one foot to the other while keeping a centered balance. Walk slowly with a sense of relaxed ease and dignity. Maintaining a stately posture, with shoulders relaxed and a soft gaze a few feet ahead without focusing on anything, but with awareness of all, will help make the experience more meditative. Walk for a period of your choosing and then stop and let yourself feel the peace of the experience.

You may want to walk outdoors on a longer familiar route that allows you to feel safe enough to have a more inward focus without being distracted by the scenery. Another idea is to walk without a goal or destination, but rather to walk more randomly in nature or around your neighborhood. Some people may choose to begin by walking fast and then to gradually slow down, letting their thoughts slow down as the walking slows down.

The most important thing is to be mindful of the body and the environment so as not to stumble or step into danger. One can synchronize breath and movement, taking several steps during each inhalation and each exhalation, paying attention to each step and each breath. Walking can also allow a person to be more attuned to the natural world. As you walk, keep your attention on your breath as well as your mantra, affirmation, or chant if you are doing one of those. You could also try singing and making up little songs and chants on your daily walks.

Years ago, my mother began a practice of walking for a mile around the apartment compound where she lived. I would imagine she was doing the walking to lose weight or enhance her physical health, but she also noticed an added benefit. She told me "I don't know what this walking is really doing for me, but I feel so noble when I am walking." So, in fact, a walking meditation can add to the stately and noble sense of who we are as divine beings.

Walking a Labyrinth with Mindfulness

Walking a labyrinth is a form of walking meditation that can symbolize a journey to the center of oneself. A labyrinth is not a maze. It is not a mystery or a puzzle to be solved. There is only a single path which leads one ever deeper into the center of the spiritual spiral. Once one has reached the center, the path leads back again to the outer world.

The labyrinth is an archetype found in many religious traditions and it dates back thousands of years. Entering the labyrinth, one steps into a sacred space. While walking the labyrinth, one can also be mindful of walking and breathing. When the center is reached, there can be an acknowledgment of the moment, a pause, a prayer, and then one turns and slowly navigates the path back to the outside world.

Mindfulness Exercises

- Mindful Exercise 1:
  Walk mindfully around your
  neighborhood in silence.

- Mindful Exercise 2:
  Walk mindfully in nature chanting a mantra,
  toning, or humming.

- Mindful Exercise 3:
  Find a labyrinth and walk it.

- Mindful Exercise 4:
  On a picture of a labyrinth,
  follow the path with your finger.

- Mindful Exercise 5:
  Wash your dishes singing
  or toning in meditative calmness.

Tito La Rosa, Peruvian Musical Shaman

CHAPTER 15

TRANCE, RITUAL, AND CEREMONY WITH DRUMS, RATTLES, FLUTES, AND SHAKERS

Another form of musical meditation uses drums, rattles, flutes, shakers, and the human voice to help a person go into a trance state. This process may involve a guide, shaman, or medicine person who is trained in leading and transforming energy. It may also be self-generated. Indigenous people from all over the world have used sacred ceremonies to assist in the elevation of consciousness, and in this day and age, many are revisiting these ancient practices and modernizing them to fit current needs. Thus, depending on the practitioners, a ceremony may involve elaborate traditional rituals or it may be expressed in meaningful modern ways.

Relationship with Instruments

A number of years ago, Dean and I interviewed the Peruvian musician, Tito La Rosa for our *Sonic Healing: Meet the Masters Video Course*. Tito La Rosa is a musical shaman who has very direct and personal relationships with his instruments. He uses drums, rattles, shakers, flutes, whistles, and water vessels to create a sound healing environment that helps people reach a deeply meditative state. His relationships with his instruments and their functions are deeply connected with, and reflective of, the elements of Earth,

Water, Fire, Air, and Sound. In ancient Peru, the instruments themselves were considered to be alive and to have a unique spirit of their own related to their form and function. For instance, blowing on the conch shell calls forth or invokes energies. A flute made from the bone of the condor may be used to call in the spirits. The whistle jar is an instrument used for going within. Feathered panpipes may be used to cleanse and purify, and so on. Each instrument has its own energy and use.

Native Americans beat on round drums or hand drums, and they chant together. From ancient times to this day, both women and men have played frame drums and participated in religious rites. Tribal people of all nations dance to the rhythm of rattles and drums, and they are able to lose themselves as their movement entrains with the rhythm. Tibetan monks may blow into long temple trumpets and crash cymbals together in order to shake up and cleanse the current vibrational field. All these practices and chanting prepare the way for more elevated meditation experiences, even though some of the sounds may seem less than meditative.

Trance Meditation Practices

- Practice 1:
  Hit a round drum with your hand or a padded drumstick
  in sync with your heartbeat for one minute or more.
  Healthy heart rate is 50-70 beats per minute.

- Practice 2:
  Use a rattle and shake it over all parts of your body
  starting with your feet and legs, then moving up
  to shake it across your torso, shoulders, arms,
  and then around your head.
  Listen to the sounds of the rattle
  as you exhale your breath and release any locked in energy.

- Practice 3:
  Join in with others who are drumming or chanting,
  and connect with their energy.

Dean Evenson playing flute with April Which–ta–lum on drum

CHAPTER 16
PRACTICE MAKES PERFECT

What Is the Benefit of a Regular Meditation Practice?

When we do something religiously, it means we do it regularly and frequently. Dean's mother, who lived to the ripe young age of 99, read the Bible and prayed every day. She did it 'religiously,' and it benefitted her inner soul. When an athlete trains in a sport, we know how important regular practice is before the big game. A musician practices their instrument daily in order to become a better player. So, when we are learning meditation, we need to commit to practicing on a regular basis. It is helpful to set aside a regular time to sit in meditation for at least 20 minutes a day. Developing the 'habit' of meditating will go a long way. If we can sit more than once a day, perhaps morning and evening, we will have even greater access to the jewels of the meditation experience.

When a woman is learning the natural childbirth process of delivery, she practices a lot of breathing so she can deal with the pain of her contractions. It is ideal if she can practice months before she actually goes into labor because if she has not fully incorporated the breathing into her very being, when those contractions begin, she will do what is typical – clench her teeth and tighten her muscles, causing her to experience more pain than necessary. On the other hand, if she had practiced her breathing, she would have access to its calming and concentrating effects, which would help her deal more effectively with the pain of her labor. It is fascinating to realize that the breathing techniques used by a modern woman in labor and a yogi are quite similar. Both involve rhythmic breathing patterns and concentration leading to an ability to overcome pain and enter a state of elevated consciousness. The result of one is birth of a new baby. The result of the other can be the birth of a new being within oneself.

A meditation practice includes a lot of breathing and breath awareness. When one is first beginning, it may seem complicated and difficult to remember what to do. That is why we encourage you to set up and stick to a regular practice in order to continuously improve your meditation experience. A benefit of having practiced your meditation over many months or years is that, if or when you should find yourself in a difficult situation of high stress, you will have access to the peaceful state of inner balance that will allow you to be in a much better position to navigate any challenges that might come up in your life. Challenges aside, your life in general will be more peaceful, enjoyable, and fulfilling and you will be more effective in achieving the life goals you set for yourself.

10 Simple Steps to Develop A Daily Meditation Practice:

1. Decide what you are willing to do every day.
2. Choose a comfortable place to practice.
3. Create an environment that supports your practice.
4. Set an intention to do it regularly.
5. Be realistic in what you are able to commit to.
6. Eliminate distractions. Turn off the phone and computer.
7. Let your family or roommates know not to disturb you.
8. Start small and let your practice grow.
9. Keep a journal and document your progress.
10. If you miss a day, get back to it soon and make a habit of it.

Silence

"Be still and know that I am God."
—Psalm 46:10, Old Testament (KJV)

We have covered a lot of material here about using sounds, songs, tones, mantra, and recorded music to support our meditation practice. All of these tools are helpful for quieting our busy minds. When all is said and done, what we are really aiming toward is ultimate stillness, the purity of a quiet mind. Even this has a natural connection with music, as expressed in the following quotation:

"It's really the space between the notes
that makes the music you enjoy so much.
Without the spaces, all you would have
is one continuous, noisy note…
Everything that's created comes out of silence.
Your thoughts emerge from the nothingness of silence.
Your words come out of this void.
Your very essence emerges from emptiness."
—Wayne W. Dyer

Now, after all this study of music and meditation, we leave you with this thought. May you come to know the restorative power of inner silence. Just as people fast by taking a break from eating, you may wish to take a break from speaking and try a day or a period of time where you abstain from speaking. It may be difficult at first, but with practice, silence can be a great healer. We love this quote, again showing the interconnectedness of music and silence:

"After silence, that which comes nearest
to expressing the inexpressible is music."
—Aldous Huxley

Inner Peace Affirmation

Repeat to yourself either silently or out loud:

I allow myself to go to a place deep inside where peace resides.

I lovingly let go of disturbing thoughts
and feelings that are holding me back.

I forgive people and events that
may have caused me pain in the past.

As I forgive and let go, I notice a sense of comfort surrounding
me and replacing any negativity with positive feelings.

I sink deeper into this experience of peace and security.

I feel a sense of trust and acceptance growing within me.

I am learning to connect with my inner core of peace
even when events and people around me feel overwhelming.

I feel joy in the realization that inner peace is always
available to me, no matter what is happening in the world.

Intention and Meaning

In closing we want to remind you that beyond the tools, techniques, chants, and mantras, the essence is the meaning you put into your meditation time. Your intention is the driving force of your creative expression, the 'why' of your life. Therefore, cultivate what is meaningful. Spend time alone or with loved ones. Enjoy yourself. It is a serious endeavor we are engaged with, this thing called life, but it's okay to be happy. What we care about and the values we have exist within a fantastic interplay of forms and functions. When we can draw from the deep source of our life-affirming values, we will be much happier, and so will everyone in our world.

We hope you have enjoyed learning about the principles of meditation and the sound tools that can be used to enhance and deepen your experience. We have probably given you more information than you need, so try things out and pick and choose what works best for you. Meditation should bring peace of mind, so please don't stress trying to absorb more than you need at the moment. The most important thing is to develop a consistent, daily meditation practice, no matter how long. As you develop your practice, you will naturally want to devote more time to it and your life will be richer for it. We look forward to hearing from you and welcome your comments, feedback, and questions. We wish you blessings on your process of finding inner peace and hopefully we will meet in person some day on this magnificent journey of life.

ACKNOWLEDGMENTS

As with any productive life that is well lived for over 70 years, we know we could not have accomplished any of this without the help of many people. We honor and appreciate the family, friends, and collaborators who have been so influential in bringing this and our many other works to see the light of day.

First and foremost, we appreciate our three children who, while growing up, put up with our alternative lifestyle and allowed us to focus on our music and our business. You are the greatest treasure of our lives. With all our travels, we may not have had a normal family life, but we did have dinner together almost every night. Cristen Olsen, Sarah Evenson, and Elijah Evenson – you are our greatest blessing, and we love you with all our hearts. We also honor our one and only granddaughter, Cybele Olsen, for her wisdom and creativity. We know you will carry on the legacy we have begun.

We honor our parents for giving us life and guidance: Dean's folks Arthur and Margaret Evenson; Dudley's folks William and Dorothy Dickinson. We may not have followed the paths you would have expected of us, but we have stayed true to the values you instilled in us. We also thank our siblings for helping us along the way: Dudley's sister Sarah Guitart, who helped edit this book; Dudley's brothers Jeff Dickinson and Bill Dickinson, and their spouses, Priscilla Dickinson and Mary Jo Dickinson; and Dean's brother Don Evenson and his partner Laura Nielsen, who sold our music at the many craft fairs and arts festivals over the years. These gatherings are where they set up a booth and made sure people heard the peaceful sounds of our Soundings of the Planet musical offerings.

We honor and appreciate the first civil rights workers, peace activists, environmentalists, and spiritual leaders including Martin Luther King, Jr., Mahatma Gandhi, Nelson Mandela, Desmond Tutu, Maya Angelou, Thich Nhat Hanh, Al Gore, and so many others who paved the way for us to create a world of our choosing. We honor Jesus, Buddha, and all the inspired

Facing page (clockwise from top left): His Holiness the Dalai Lama; Soundings Arizona Team 1990s; Dudley, Dean, Ram Dass; Pandit Shivnath Mishra, Dean, Deobrat Mishra; Dean, Cybele Olsen, Cristen Olsen, Dudley; Dean, Swami Satchidananda; Cha-das-ska-dum Which-ta-lum, Dean; Dean, Naomi Judd, Dudley; Soundings Washington Team 2012; Sarah Evenson, Kent Johnson, Dudley, Cybele Olsen, David Olsen, Cristen Olsen, Elijah Evenson, Dean; Li Xiangting; Sarah Evenson, Elijah Evenson, Cristen Olsen; Dudley, Jack Canfield; Dudley, Cristen Olsen, Elijah Evenson, Sarah Evenson; Dudley, Joan Borysenko, Deepak Chopra, Dean; Soundings Washington Team 2002; Dean, d'Rachael; Tom Barabas; Larry Dossey, Barbara Dossey, Dean; Jonathan Kramer; Scott Huckabay; Dudley, Dean, Iyanla Vanzant

beings who preceded us on this journey. We appreciate Baba Ram Dass who let us record his early lectures which inspired us to launch our record label, Soundings of the Planet. We thank Peggy Hitchcock and Sky Crosby for letting us park our bus on their land, which gave us the space to focus on our video work, and eventually to launch Soundings of the Planet. Also, great appreciation to Richie Chapin, who let us set up our first booth at the Tanque Verde Swap Meet in Tucson, which got us going on selling our music directly to the public.

We honor the 14th Dalai Lama of Tibet who allowed us to use his *Green Tara Mantra* on our album *Prayer: A Multicultural Journey of Spirit.* And we're grateful for the many times we were in his presence videotaping his compassionate wisdom. The picture of him tugging on Dean's beard is one of my most memorable photographs! We honor Paul Horn who first played flute in the Taj Mahal and opened our world to meditation music. We also thank John Denver for inviting Dean to perform with him at the Pine Ridge Reservation as well as the Rio Earth Summit. Special gratitude goes to Louise Hay who inspired so many of us with her guided affirmations. Dean is grateful for his flute teacher, Irving Kafka, who taught him for ten years and then told him not to try to make a living making music. It's just as well that advice didn't stick.

Our hands are up to our Native American brothers, sisters, and elders who have shown us a path of honoring and respecting our Mother Earth. We are grateful that Stewart Brand, founder of the Whole Earth Catalogue, had the vision in 1972 to send 15 Native Americans to the first United Nations Conference on the Human Environment in Stockholm, Sweden, where we met with them and videotaped them sharing their wisdom which we have carried with us throughout our lives. Great honor goes to the keepers of the Hopi prophecy David Monongye and Thomas Banyacya, Shoshone spokesman Rolling Thunder, and many others. From his video work at Wounded Knee, Dean met John Fire Lame Deer, Frank Fools Crow, and Rod Skenandore who helped to shape our path. We honor Gwich'in Indian, Sarah James, for her tireless work defending the Arctic National Wildlife Refuge (ANWR) from oil drilling. Our connections with Jewell James and Cha-das-ska-dum Which-ta-lum of the Lummi Tribe, and more recently Freddie Lane, have inspired us to focus our activism locally and keep holding strong for the planet. A shout out to all the Water Protectors who took a stand in solidarity with the Standing Rock tribe resisting yet another pipeline.

We offer our boundless gratitude to the many musicians we have collaborated with over the years in sharing our Peace Through Music mission. This illustrious list in part includes: Tom Barabas, d'Rachael, Scott Huckabay, Li Xiangting, Deobrat Mishra, Pt. Shivnath Mishra, Fumio, Gordy Schaeffer (SoulFood), Daniel Paul, Phil Heaven, Sarah Evenson (our daughter), Tim Alexander, Jeff Willson, Peter Ali, Singh Kaur (aka Lorellei), Don Reeve, Beth Quist, Doug Tessler, Henry Han, Walter Makichen, Jonathan Kramer, Natalie Twigg, Chris Hawkins, Aziz and Khabira Paige, Gregg Callahan, A.B., Cyrille Verdeaux, Burke Mulvany, Gina Salá, Jason Darling, Richard Hardy, Sergey Kuryokhin, Vladimir Solyanik, Fantuzzi, and Sananda, to name a few. We are grateful for the collective, creative collaboration, and friendship of all that have made the music come alive and help so many people.

We couldn't have done any of this without the amazing Soundings teams who helped guide the business aspects of our record label. First was my brother, Bill Dickinson, and his then-girlfriend, Jane Harris, who showed up at our door in Tucson ready to help turn our music offerings into a proper business. Jane stayed on for many years and helped run Soundings. Over the decades we have had hundreds of people keeping the business going. Ariel Hancock, Don Karl, Serene Stevenson, Liz Hjelmseth, Randy Hock, and Stephanie LeBlanc also helped manage. When we needed a clone of Dean, Phil Heaven moved in next door, and he has been managing the Soundings Studio and business ever since. He's the best problem solver, has perfect pitch, plays viola on many of our recordings, and is an ardent composer and producer. We give special thanks to our everything supporter, Brett Steelhammer, who keeps our Soundings of the Planet YouTube Channel and social media engaged and nudges me to do all I should be doing. Gratitude as well to Jon Carroll who took on the organizing of our vast video archive and was our representative at Standing Rock.

We thank Scott Blum and Madisyn Taylor, founders of DailyOM, for seeing our potential and helping us launch our successful online courses on meditation, music, and sound healing.

We are grateful that Naomi Judd discovered our music, used it in her healing process, and loved it enough to hand it out to people she met along her tours. We thank those authors who welcomed us to play our music live and do our meditations before or during their presentations including Deepak Chopra, Joan Borysenko, Larry Dossey, Iyanla Vanzant, Denise Linn, Lillias Folan, Judith Orloff, and don Miguel Ruiz.

Special thanks to Jack Canfield, co-author of the *Chicken Soup for the Soul* series, and my co-author in the best-selling book *The Big Secret: The World's Leading Entrepreneurs and Professionals Reveal Their Big Secrets for Achieving the Health, Wealth, and Lifestyle You Desire.*

We appreciate Arnold Patent for inviting us to record his many workshops on abundance, support, and universal principles. He helped make sense of the many new and ancient philosophies swirling into our lives. From those workshops, we branched out to significant consciousness and healing conferences and benefited from years of presenting our music at Hay House, Omega, Body & Soul, AMTA, NICABM, and other wellness, yoga, massage, psychotherapy, and spa conferences. We are grateful to have presented workshops at Kripalu, Omega, Canyon Ranch, and many other healing and massage conferences, as well as wonderful retail stores around the country large and small, who sell our music.

And now, last but not least, we give a great big thank you to the people who have helped birth this book. It was a great decision to work with Anthony J.W. Benson who has helped in endless ways to make our manuscript become a real book. Publishing a book is different from making a recording, so working with someone as creative as he, who knows the business, has been super helpful and a fun and fruitful collaboration. We are also glad to be working with our longtime graphic designer and good friend, Bob Paltrow, who has been responsible for the beautiful covers of so many of our award-winning albums and videos over the years. It is wonderful to work with such a talented person who instills confidence in the look and feel of what we are presenting. Thanks to our son Elijah Evenson, for his stunning chakra imagery.

Special thanks to Joel and Michelle Levey who agreed to write the Foreword. This amazing couple has been meditating and teaching since the '60s. At the height of their career they devoted a year to silent, solitary, contemplative practice under the sponsorship of the Dalai Lama, with the intention of being of greater service when they returned to their outer work in the world. Now that is a commitment to focusing on tuning your instrument to let the music of your life be an inspiration to all you meet in the world!

We are deeply grateful to Paul Russell and Jane Harris for taking on the editing in such a detailed way. And for other editors and readers who helped clarify and catch errors, thanks to Cami Ostman, Sarah Guitart, Brett Steelhammer, and Troy H. B. We also very much appreciate the many authors, teachers, and new thought leaders who offered their testimonials ahead of publication.

Finally, to all of you who are reading our words and who listen to our music, you are the reason we do what we do. Thank you all!

Meditation Moment
Dudley Evenson
52 weekly guided affirmations
Music by Dean & Dudley Evenson

Dean & Dudley Evenson Present
healing the holy land
a Musical Journey of Faith
soundings of the planet

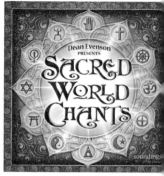

Dean Evenson PRESENTS
SACRED WORLD CHANTS
soundings of the planet

Ocean Dreams
Dean Evenson
soundings of the planet

DEAN EVENSON   WALTER MAKICHEN
Golden Spa Tones
TIBETAN SINGING BOWLS WITH FLUTE & OCEAN
soundings of the planet

CHAKRA healing

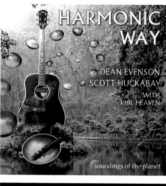

HARMONIC WAY
DEAN EVENSON
SCOTT HUCKABAY
WITH PHIL HEAVEN
soundings of the planet

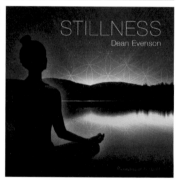

STILLNESS
Dean Evenson

CHAKRA
MEDITATIONS & TONES
DUDLEY & DEA EVENSON
soundings of the planet

DEAN & DUDLEY EVENSON PRESENT
SONIC HEALING
Meet the Masters Video Course
music | meditation | sound | healing
10 HOUR-LONG VIDEO PROGRAMS
featuring 30 MUSICIANS, DOCTORS, RESEARCHERS, AUTHORS, THERAPISTS, PIONEERS
soundings of the planet

DEAN & DUDLEY EVENSON
4 EARTH
SCENIC VISTAS OF OCEAN STREAM RIVER POND
soundings of the planet

DEAN & DUDLEY EVENSON
MEDITATION MOODS
soundings of the planet
SCENIC VISTAS FOR AN INNER JOURNEY

QUIETING THE MONKEY MIND: HOW TO MEDITATE WITH MUSIC RESOURCES

For additional resources & links visit:
www.soundings.com/meditation-resources

A Short Selection of Music and Videos by Dudley and Dean Evenson

Meditation Music:

Chakra Healing
Desert Dawn Song
Golden Spa Tones
Harmonic Way
Healing Sanctuary
Meditation Moods
Ocean Dreams
Sacred Earth
Stillness

Guided Affirmations:

A Sound Sleep: Guided Meditations & Nature Sounds
Chakra Meditations & Tones
Meditation Moment: 52 Weekly Affirmations

Chant and Mantra Music:

Arctic Refuge: A Gathering of Tribes
Healing the Holy Land
Native Healing
Prayer: A Musical Journey of Spirit
Sacred World Chants

Videos:

4 Earth: Scenic Vistas of Ocean, Stream, River, Pond
A Year of Guided Meditations
Eagle River
Meditation Moods
Sonic Healing Meet the Masters Video Course

Selected Books by Authors and Teachers:

Andrew Cohen—*Living Enlightenment*
Andrew Weil—*Eight Weeks to Optimum Health*
Anodea Judith—*Wheels of Life*
Arinna Weisman and Jean Smith—*The Beginners Guide to Insight Meditation*
B.K.S. Iyengar—*Light on the Yoga Sutras of Patanjali*
Baba Ram Dass—*Be Here Now*
Christine Stevens—*Music Medicine*
Cyndi Dale—*The Subtle Body: An Encyclopedia of Your Energetic Anatomy*
Deanna Minich—*Whole Detox: A 21 Day Personalized Program*
Deepak Chopra—*Ageless Body, Timeless Mind*
Don Miguel Ruiz—*The Four Agreements*
Eckhart Tolle—*The Power of Now*
Ed and Deb Shapiro—*The Unexpected Power of Mindfulness & Meditation*
Edgar Cayce—*There Is a River*
Eleanor H. Porter—*Pollyanna*
Hazrat Inayat Khan—*The Mysticism of Sound and Music*
His Holiness the 14th Dalai Lama—*The Heart of Meditation*
Ilona Selke—*Dream Big: The Universe is Listening*
Jack Canfield—*The Success Principles*
Jack Kornfield—*A Path with Heart*
James Finley—*Christian Meditation: Experiencing the Presence of God*
James K. Papp—*Inquire Within: A Guide to Living in Spirit*
James O'Dea—*Soul Awakening Practice*
Jeff Foster—*The Deepest Acceptance*
Joan Borysenko—*Minding the Body, Mending the Mind*
Joel Kramer—*The Passionate Mind*
Joel Levey and Michelle Levey—*Living in Balance*
John Selby—*Quiet Your Mind*
Jon Kabat-Zinn—*Wherever You Go There You Are*
Jonathan Ellerby—*Return to the Sacred*
Jonathan Goldman and Andi Goldman—*The Humming Effect*
Joseph S. Benner—*The Impersonal Life*
Joshua Leeds—*The Power of Sound*
Larry Dossey—*Healing Words: The Power of Prayer and the Practice of Medicine*
Laurel Elizabeth Keyes—*Toning: The Creative Power of the Voice*
Layne Redmond—*When the Drummers Were Women*

Louise Hay—*You Can Heal Your Life*
Madisyn Taylor—*Daily OM: Learning to Live*
Marcus Aurelius—*Meditations*
Matt Kahn—*Whatever Arises, Love That*
Michael Bernard Beckwith—*Spiritual Liberation*
Osho (aka Rajneesh)—*Meditation: The First and Last Freedom*
Pema Chodron—*How to Meditate*
Rabbi David A. Cooper—*Kaballah Meditation*
Robert Gass—*Chanting: Discovering Spirit in Sound*
Ron Roth—*The Healing Path of Prayer*
Rumi—*The Illuminated Rumi with Coleman Barks & Michael Green*
Russill Paul—*The Yoga of Sound*
Steven Halpern—*Sound Health*
Swami Satchidananda—*Intregral Yoga Hatha*
Tara Brach—*Radical Acceptance*
Thich Nhat Hanh—*Living Buddha, Living Christ*
Thomas Ashley-Ferrand—*Healing Mantras*
Wayne W. Dyer—*Change Your Thoughts – Change Your Life*
Yogananda—*Autobiography of a Yogi*
Yogi Bhajan—*The Chakras: Kundalini Yoga*

Meditation, Yoga, and Retreat Centers:

Blue Spirit—Nosara, Costa Rica
Breitenbush Hot Springs—Detroit, OR
Cloud Mountain—Castle Rock, WA
Esalen—Big Sur, CA
Hollyhock—Cortez Island, BC, Canada
Kripalu Center for Yoga & Health—Stockbridge, MA
Omega Institute—Rhinebeck, NY
Plum Village—Loubès-Bernac, France
Self Realization Fellowship—Los Angeles, CA
Shambala Mountain Center—Red Feather Lakes, CO
Spirit Rock—Woodacre, CA
The Chopra Center—Carlsbad, CA
Upaya Zen Center—Santa Fe, NM
Yogaville—Buckingham, VA

DUDLEY AND DEAN EVENSON are respected musicians and multi-media producers who have been living their dreams for five decades since they met in 1968. During the 1970s, they lived and traveled with their young family in a half-sized, converted school bus documenting the new consciousness that was emerging. Capturing the people, places, and events of the day, their use of the newly released portable video camera placed them as trailblazers of a technological revolution that continues to this day.

In 1979, they co-founded their music label, Soundings of the Planet, with a mission of sharing Peace Through Music®. Their entrepreneurial spirit and musical talents propelled them as pioneers into the field of sound healing. Their award-winning music and videos have been used in far-ranging settings from hospitals and yoga centers to prisons, schools, homes, and workplaces to support people's healing and life process.

Over the course of many decades, the Evensons joined new thought leaders around the globe, performing concerts and presenting workshops on meditation and sound healing. By 2018, they had produced over 80 albums and numerous videos, with their music being enjoyed by millions of people worldwide. Their collaborations with outstanding musicians friends have brought forth a continuous stream of life-enhancing music with more to come and new releases every year.

These days, after years of traveling to conferences and workshops, Dudley and Dean are content to stay home, reaching out to the world via webinars, interviews, streaming music sites, and the internet. They live in a cottage by a wild river in a forested valley of the Cascade Mountains, where Dean walks to the barn studio in the morning for his daily exercise routine and to work on his music and media. Dudley practices her yoga in the house and reaches out to the world through writing, coaching, and keeping Soundings of the Planet going. Later they may meet in the garden, or take a hike across the field to the nearby river. Every night is date night. That's what happens when you marry your soul mate.

Next to the main Soundings studio in town are three houses that Dudley and Dean purchased when they first moved to Bellingham. They form a semi-intentional and exceptional community where friends, musicians, healers, gardeners, builders, entrepreneurs, artists, and filmmakers live. Dudley and Dean's collective dreams keep manifesting as peaceful music and videos continue to stream out and touch individuals around the globe.

Soundings of the Planet music and blog:
www.soundings.com • 800/93 PEACE (800/937-3223)

Social media and YouTube search:
Soundings of the Planet   Dean Evenson   Dudley Evenson

INDEX

Note: Page numbers in italics indicate photos, charts, or illustrations.

arts&culture

New Age's Old Pros

Since 1979, Bellingham's Soundings of the Planet has soothed millions of listeners.

BY JACOB UITTI

Dean and Dudley Evenson

A little yellow house sits on a patch of land about 30 minutes outside Bellingham. A few dozen feet away, the frosty Nooksack River rushes by. Thick green splotches of moss run up and down tree trunks, and the air is free from cell service. Residing in that little yellow house are Dean and Dudley Evenson, founders of the wildly successful musical business Soundings of the Planet, whose elongated, pastorally soft melodies, such as "Mending Your Own Mind" and "Gentle Season," you've likely heard on a massage table or in a yoga studio without knowing their origins.

Inside the little yellow house are also instruments—a baby grand piano, a harp, and some drums dangling from an overhang. And often music is playing; soft songs rich with strings move almost effortlessly like wind through leaves. On a flat-screen television videos play: birds landing on branches, a frog kicking its legs in clear water. This is the ambient, naturally focused world that Soundings, and its two founders, manifest.

The business began formally in 1979 when the duo created their record label outside Tucson, AZ, which has since gone on to sell millions of albums—the most famous of which include *Chakra Healing, Ocean Dreams,*

and *Healing Sanctuary*—and enjoy a similarly high number of digital streams. But in another way, the project began in 1968, the day Dean moved into Dudley's apartment building, taking the flat she'd been using as a low-key, makeshift dance and yoga room.

Dean, master's in molecular biology from the University of Maine in hand, had come to New York's East Village to learn a trade in the music business. He was already an accomplished flutist, but now wanted to become an engineer—"the guy behind the board reminding Eric Clapton his guitar is out of tune," explains Dudley, 73, looking fondly at her husband, 72, whose long white beard is marked by a thick dread down the middle.

The day the two met, their relationship took off. Meeting young in the tumultuous 1960s provided a lot of inspiration for a new couple in search of art and spirituality. At the time, Dean, along with the music trade, found himself studying filmmaking and Dudley studied photography. The two were fascinated with the newly invented portable video camera. Its freedom and populist aspect, Dudley says, provided the couple's first window into a larger purpose. "We were all about trying to put the tools of media in the hands of the people," she explains. "We believe everyone has a valid perspective and

point of view. We wanted to use the video camera to introduce people to each other."

Dean and Dudley began to travel, video camera in hand, finding gurus, speakers, and eventually Native American elders who shared with them messages about the earth as an actual living being. "That's when we really woke up," says Dean. So the two began to explore the concepts of balance, harmony, and nature. This search led them to spiritualist Ram Dass, whose lecture Dean and Dudley later recorded. They began selling cassette copies of this lecture at swap meets and craft fairs around the country, learning an important lesson: Cassettes were much easier to distribute than cumbersome reel-to-reel videotapes. Not long after, Dean began recording Soundings' first album, *Desert Dawn Song*. He slept overnight in the desert outside Tucson and recorded "the birds waking up just as I woke up," he says. "That became the base track. We used it as the inspiration to play the music."

Quickly, the Soundings nature recordings became popular at hippie venues and wellness conferences early in the New Age movement, where the couple mostly sold their work to those interested in massage, yoga, and meditation. "Our motto was peace through music," Dudley says. "People wanted

more and more of it. It helped them relax and deal with stress and chronic pain. A lot of music comes from an ego space, people wanting recognition. But our music comes from an intention of peace."

It should not be forgotten that Dean Evenson—flutist, engineer, and tinkerer—is also a scientist. One aspect of the world he most appreciates is the notion of vibrations, his understanding of which has influenced Soundings recordings. It's a bit complicated, but the basic idea is that all things can be reduced to vibrations. "Everything has its own signature vibration," Dean says. Using a scientific principle that bodies can vibrate at the same rate together, Dean composes the basic music for the recordings. The melodies rely on a subdued, even inaudible, quality that relaxes the body's vibrations and puts it in tune with the low, inaudible hum of nature, otherwise known as the alpha state. "It's very subtle," Dean says. "You don't notice it that much." In this way, the soft blanket-like music (composed without refrains and utilizing tremolo) carries Soundings' signature soothing resonance.

In the following decades, the founding parents of Soundings eventually released some 80 albums (the most recent in November), some featuring accompanying musicians (at one point Soundings employed 22 people). They've also produced countless videos, which they share on their YouTube page. The business grew in part from their regular touring and performances at the conferences (some alongside Deepak Chopra and Larry Dossey); their family did too with the introduction of three children. They all traveled the country in a bus selling tapes and CDs. Eventually, though, the Evensons landed in the Pacific Northwest, where Dean and Dudley bought a few homes, including the little yellow one.

In the late 1990s and early 2000s, however, Soundings endured the nearly devastating cratering of the music business, when CD sales plummeted after the introduction of MP3s. "There was a lot of tightening of our belts," Dudley recalls. But in the last seven years that has flipped, thanks to digital streaming. With more and more listeners finding their music online, Soundings has flourished again—almost beyond belief.

"We're doing very well," Dudley nods. Many of the streams come from Spotify and Pandora, which offer sizable direct deposits. And an upcoming project, which will likely see the light of day this year, will feature Bellingham resident Tim Alexander, drummer of famed rock band Primus (which Dudley first called "Preemus" before Dean lovingly corrected her). The project is yet another example of the effort the couple continues to put in well into their 70s. Dean and Dudley, who have always dreamed of helping people relax and heal through art, know success comes not only from spiritual inspiration. "You *do a* dream," Dudley asserts. "We were ready and willing to do the hard work." ∎

music@seattleweekly.com

SEATTLE WEEKLY • WEDNESDAY, MARCH 22, 2017   19

For press inquiries or additional information, please contact music@soundings.com

For additional resources & links visit:

www.soundings.com/quieting-monkey-mind
www.soundings.com/meditation-resources

Thank you for reviewing *Quieting the Monkey Mind* at
amazon.com, barnesandnoble.com
and other bookseller sites